Mandela & Flower

Coloring Book

Aryla Publishing 2020

978-1-912675-84-5

www.arylapublishing.com

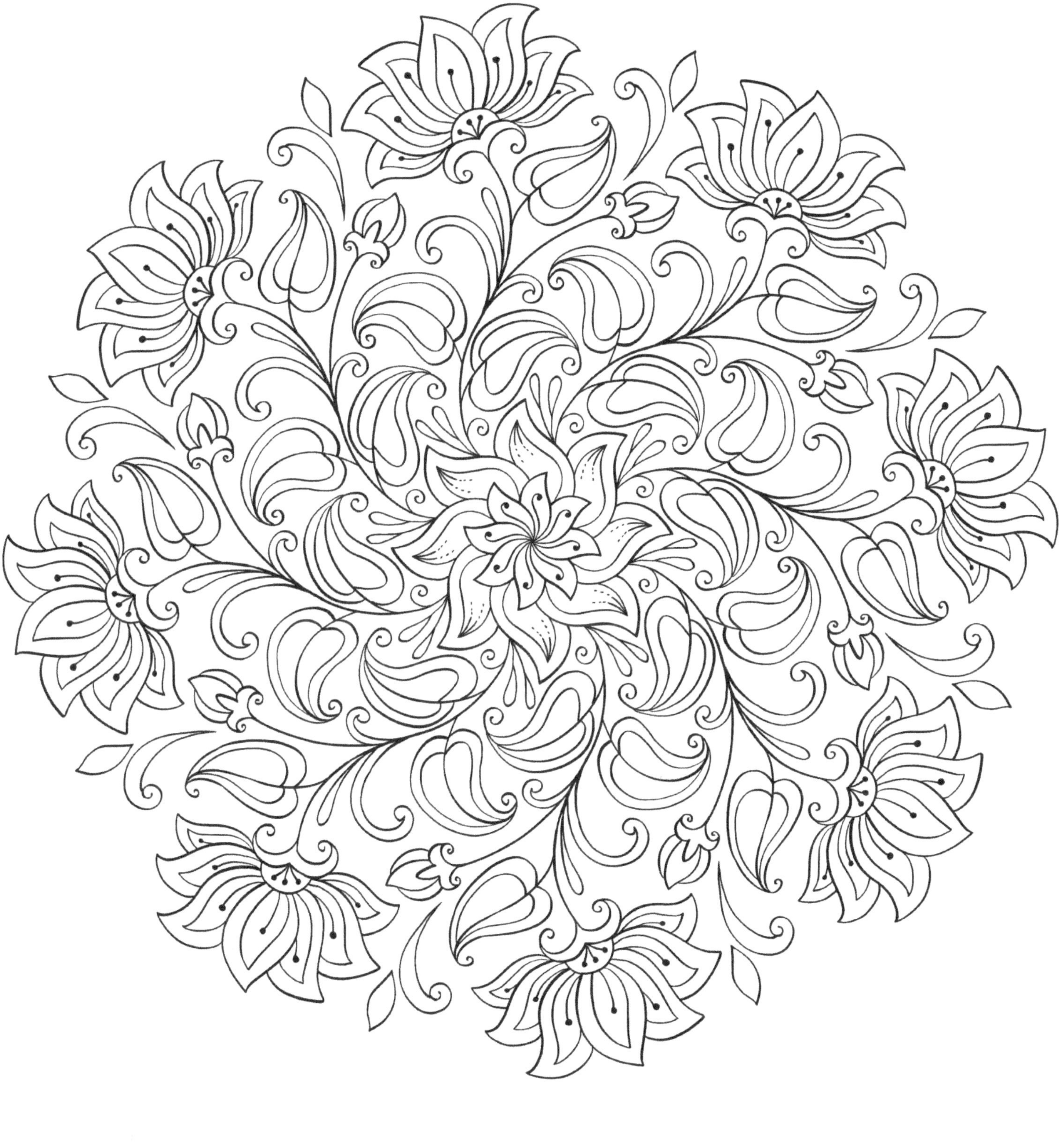

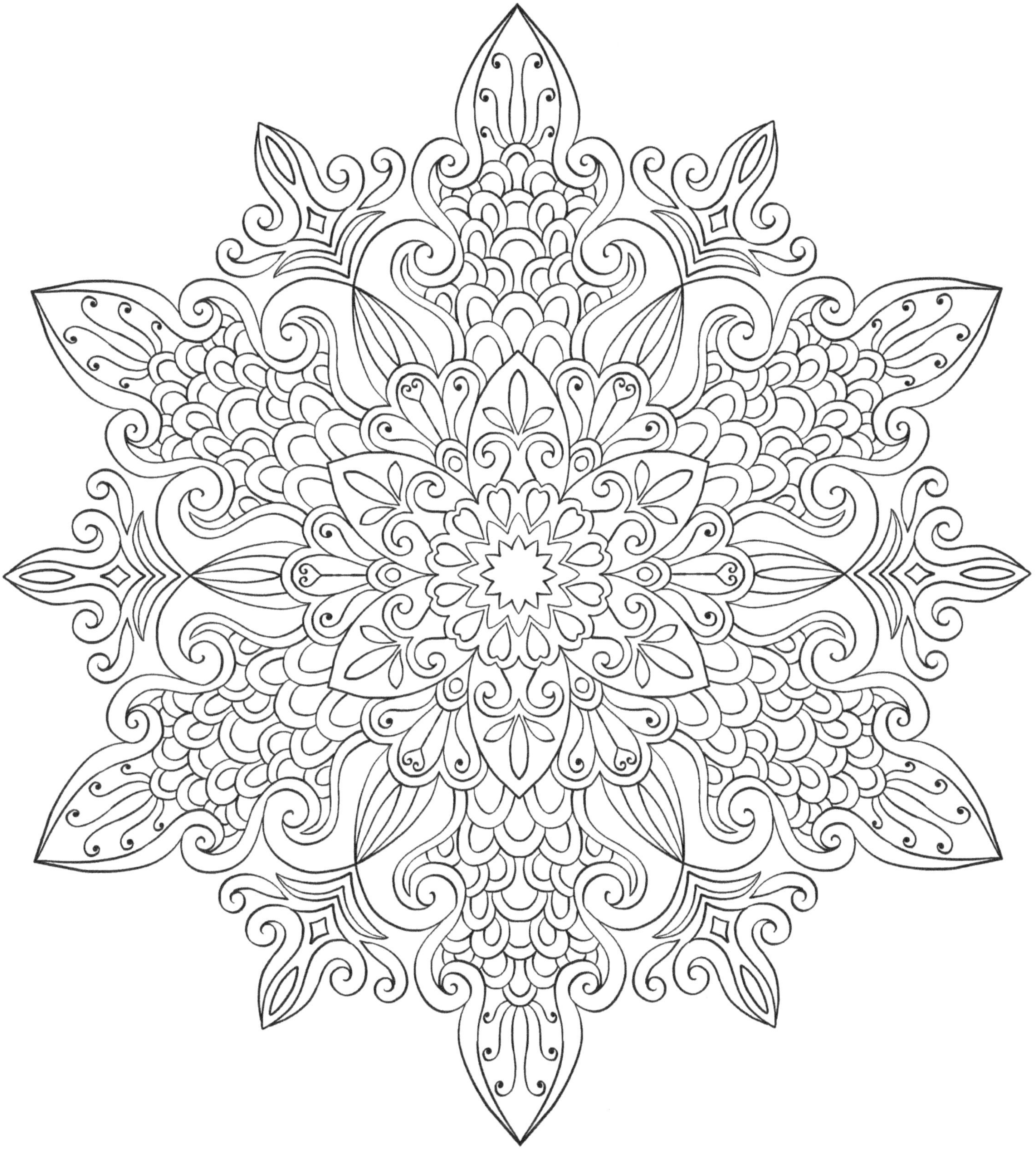

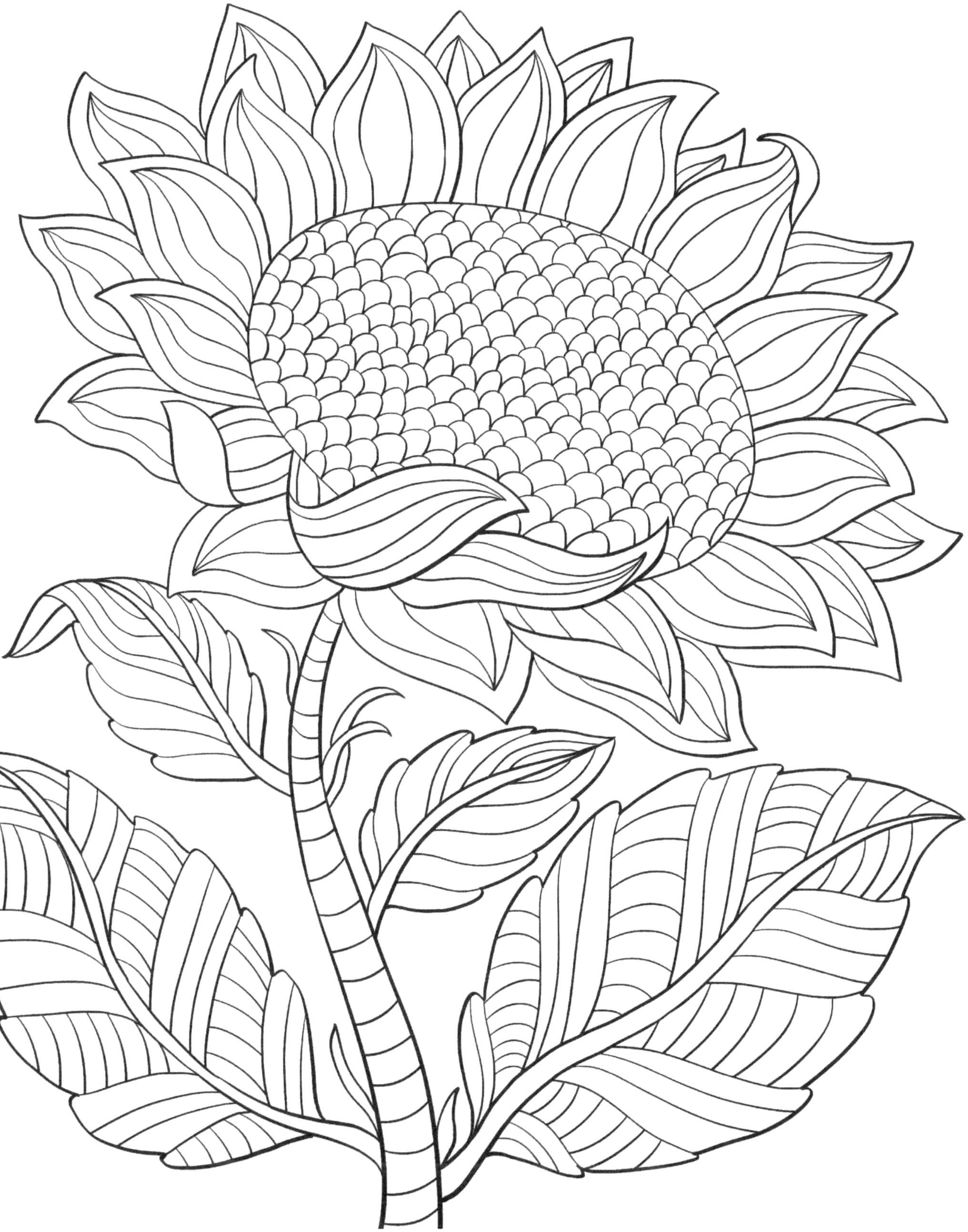

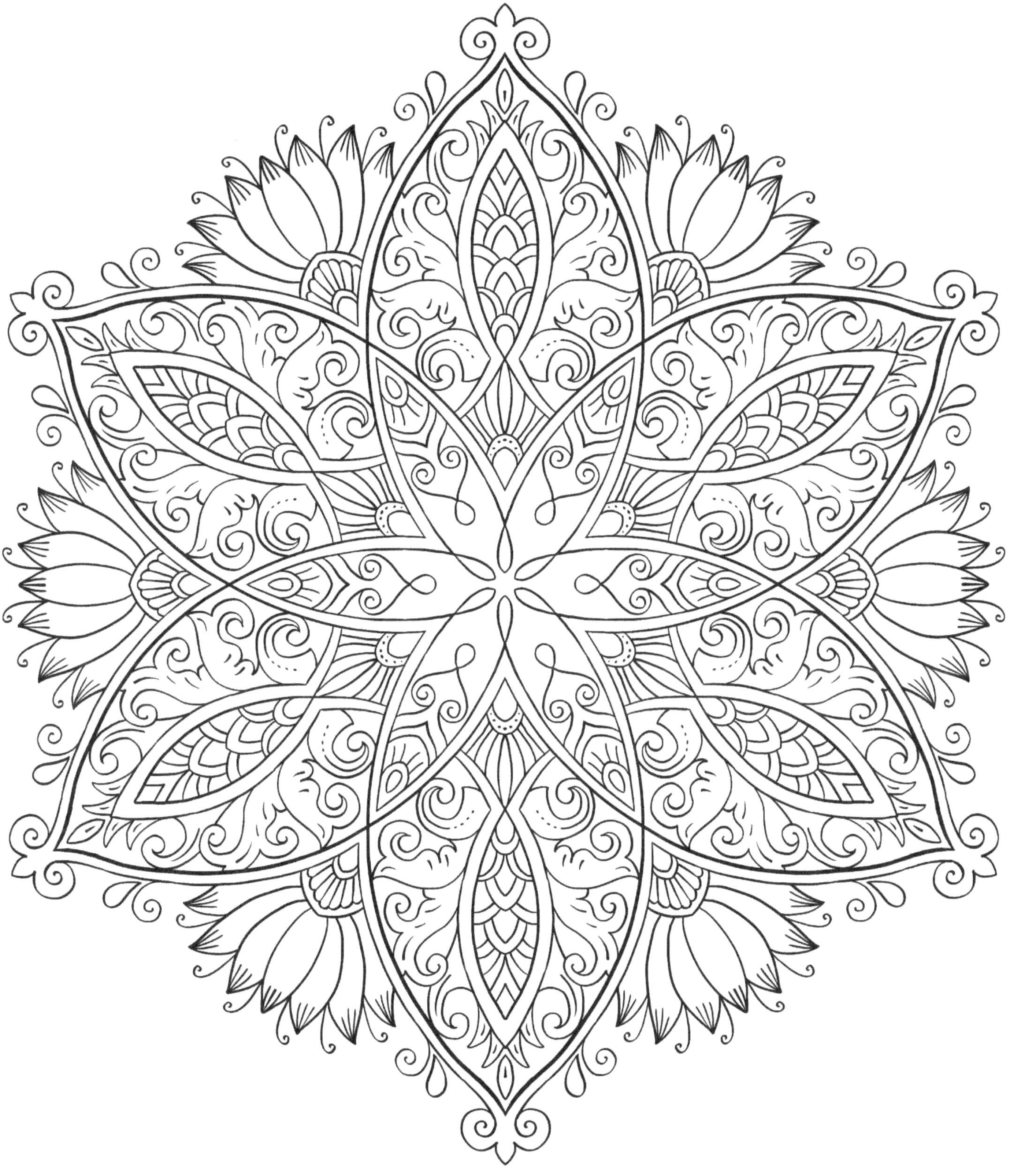

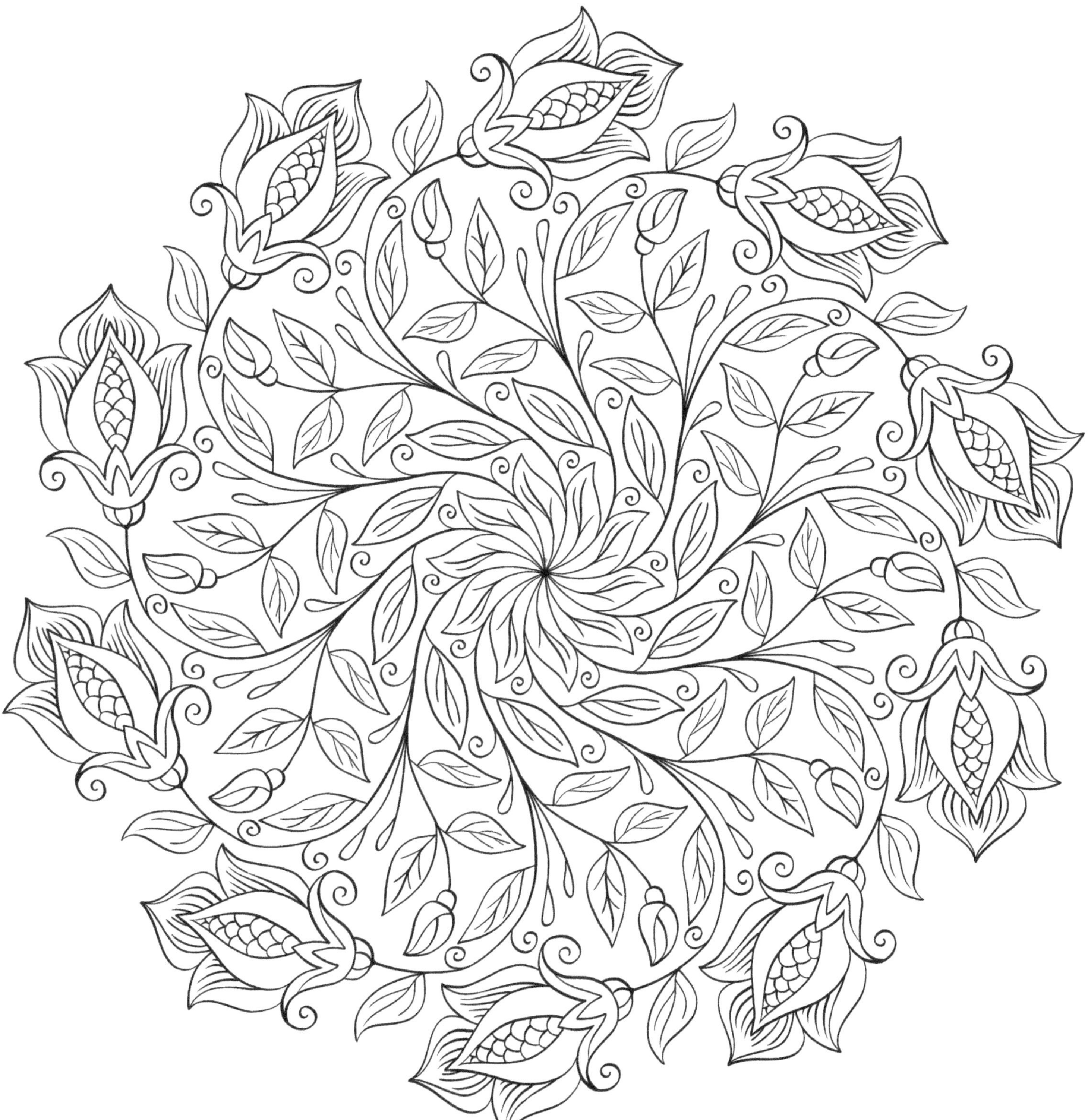

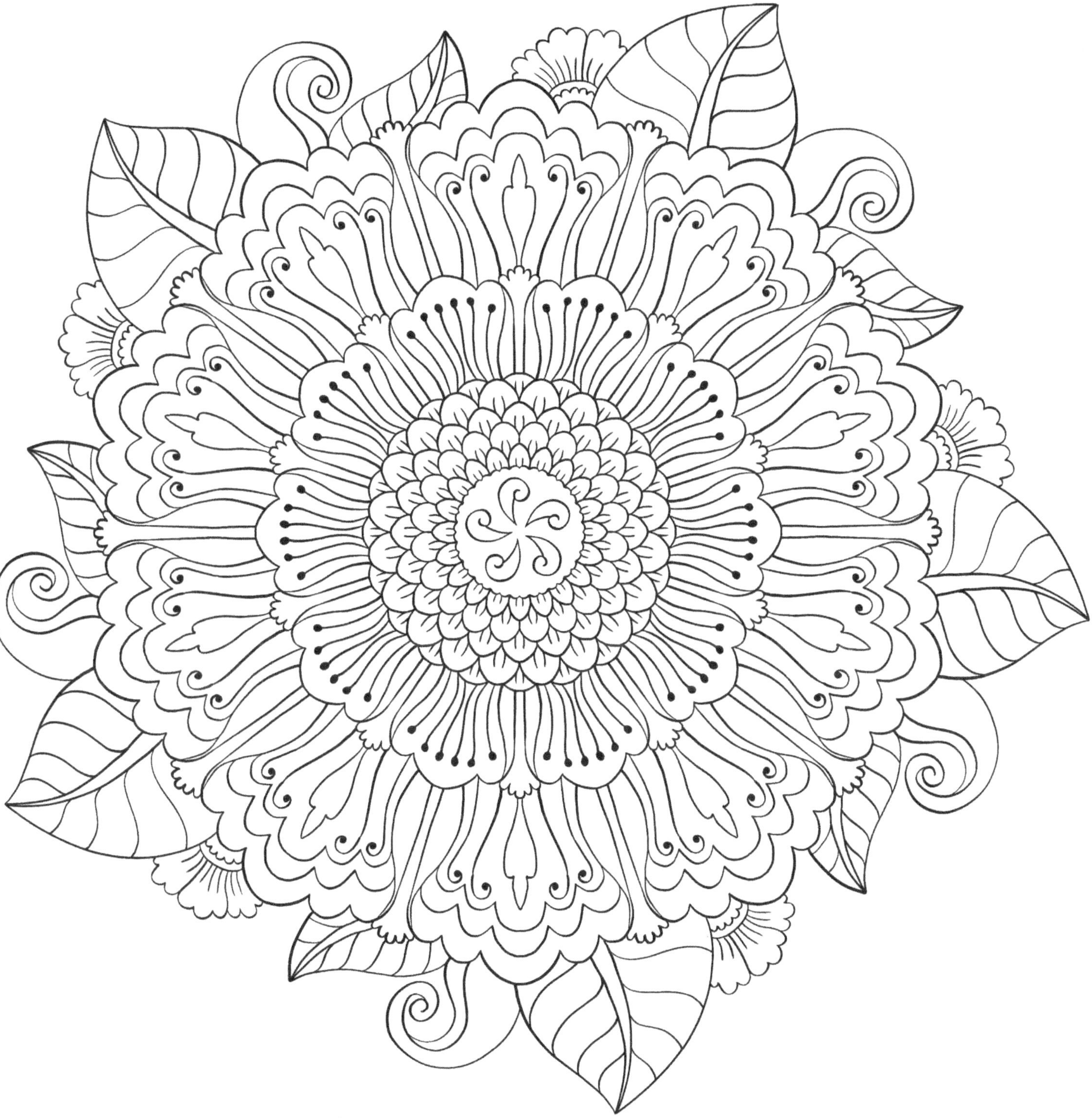

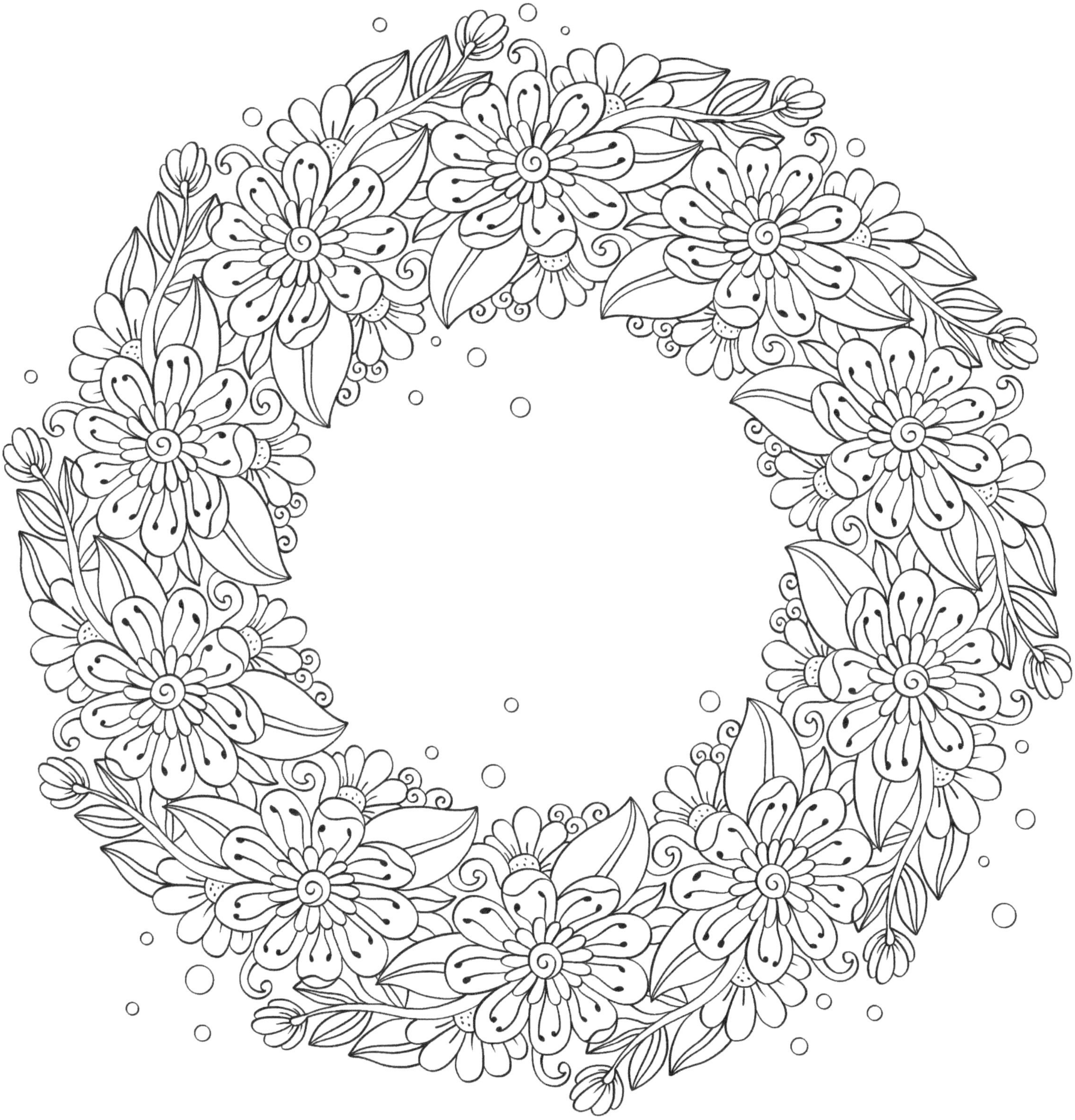

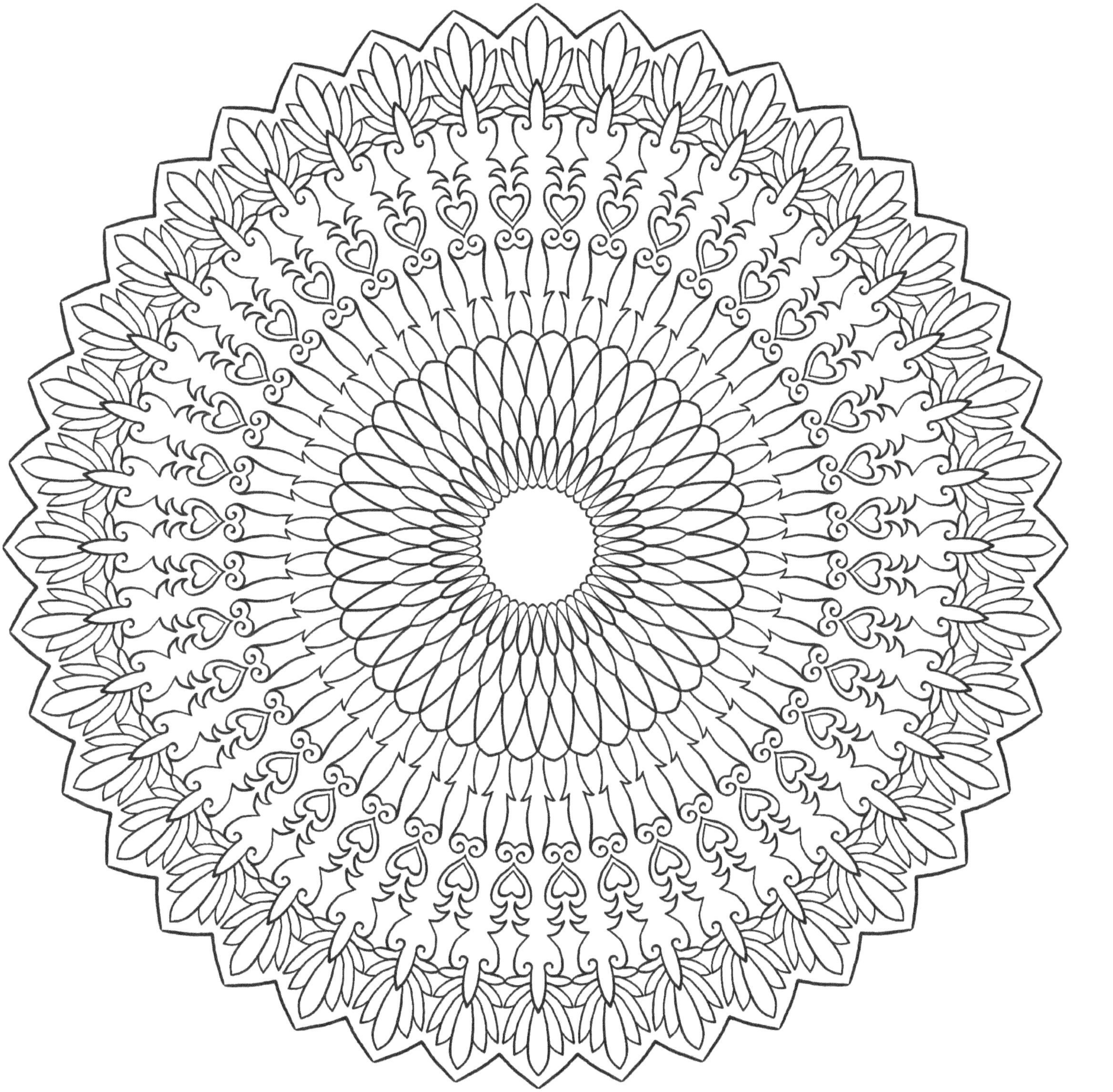

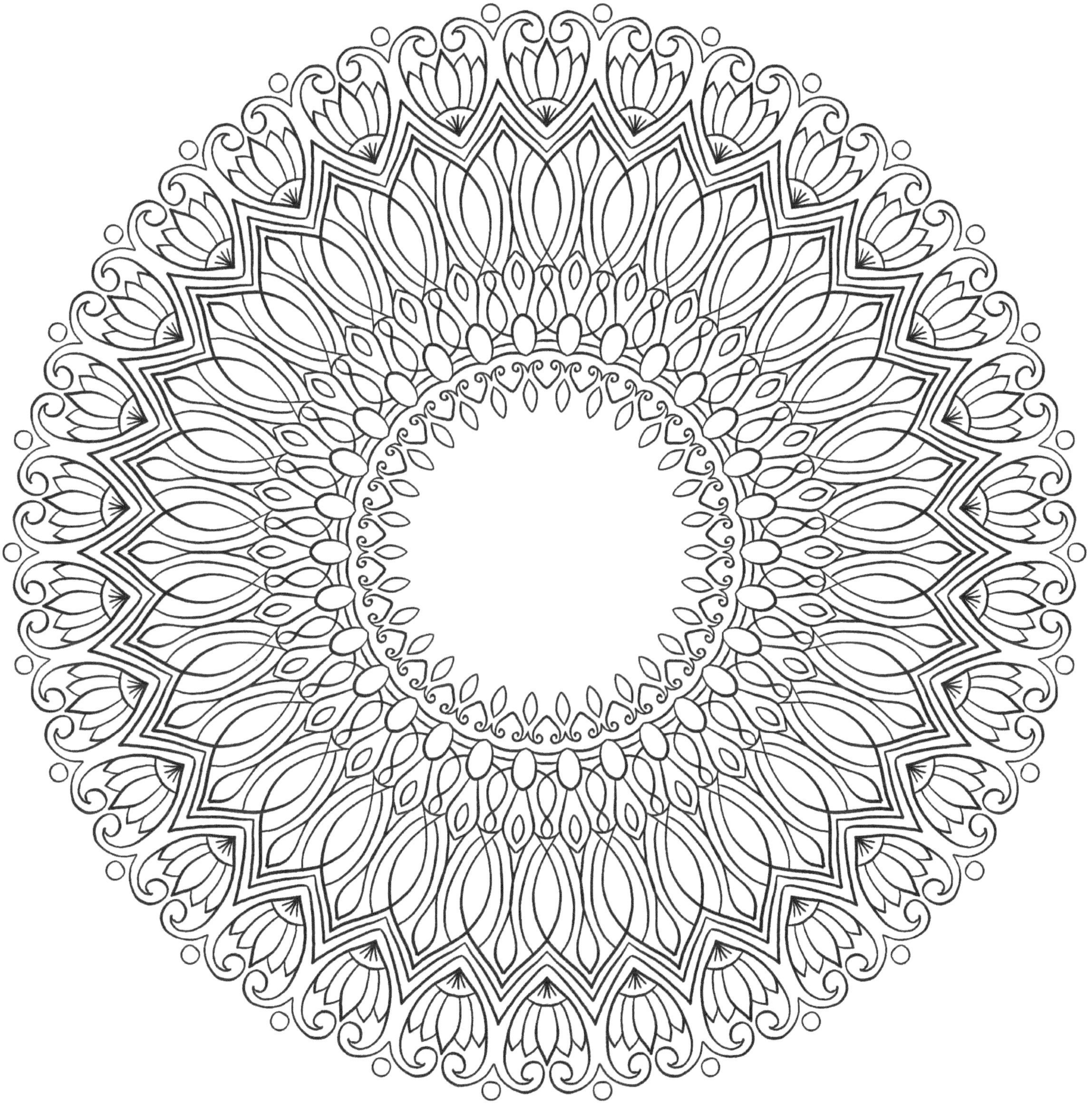

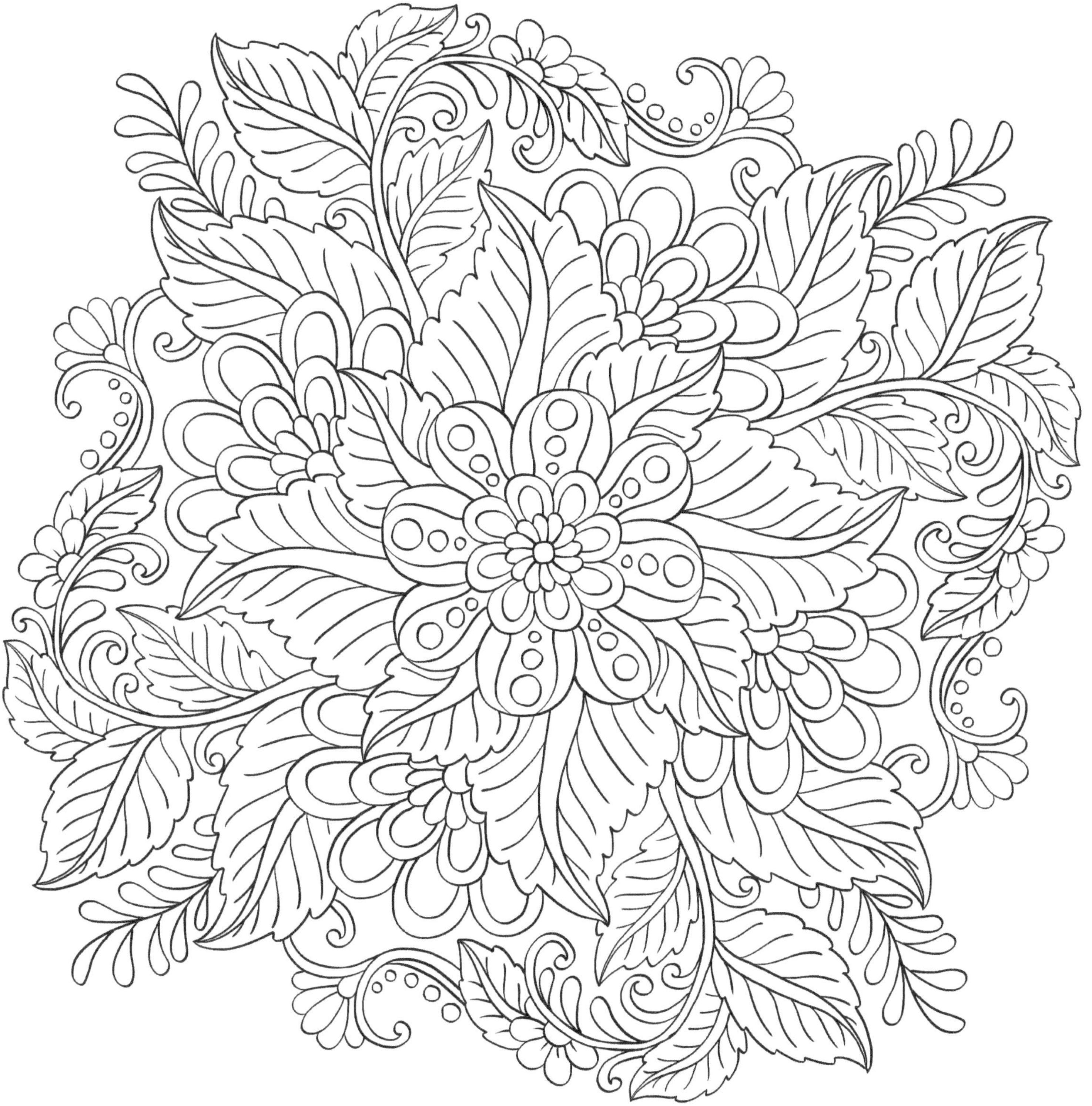

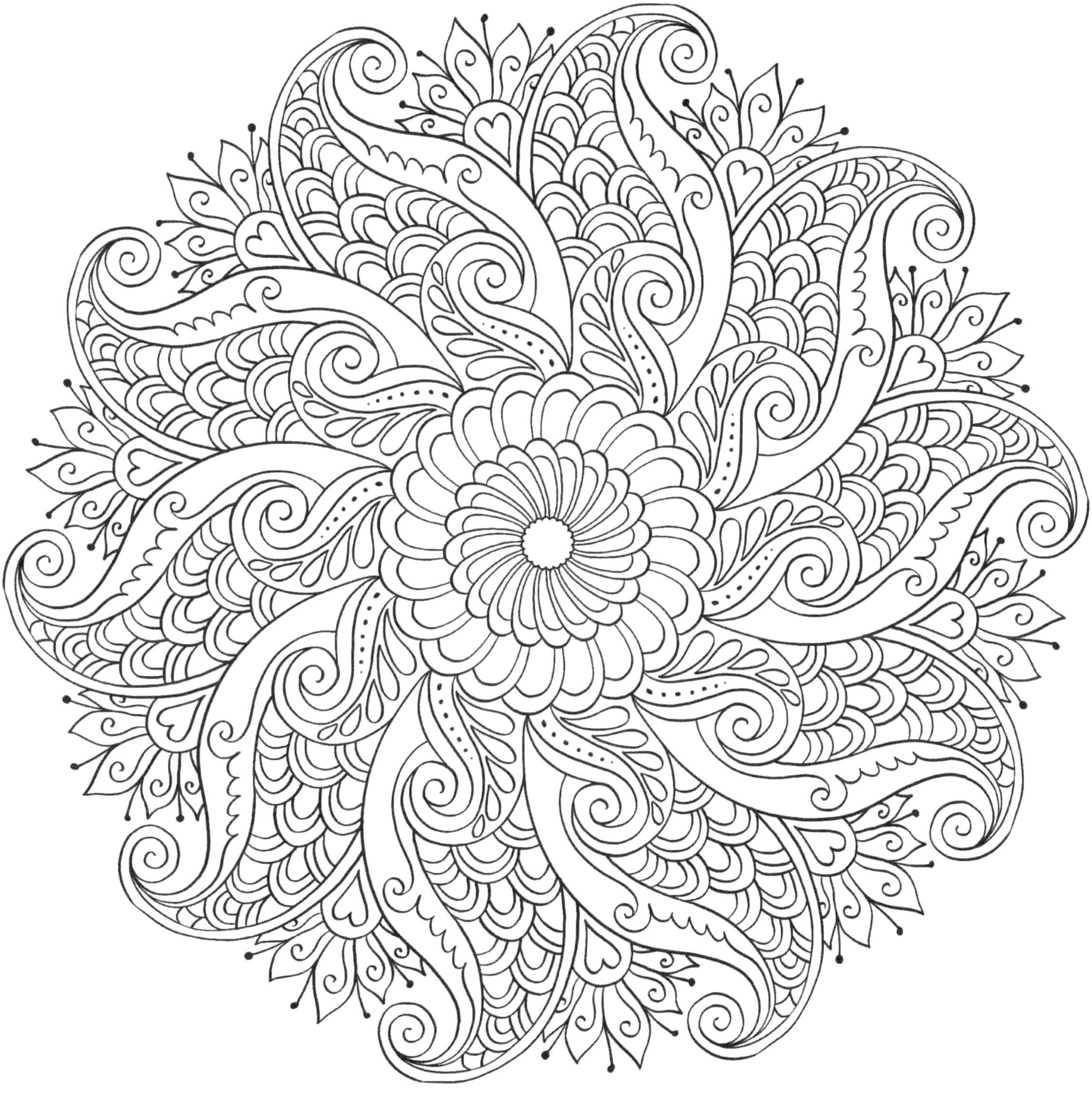

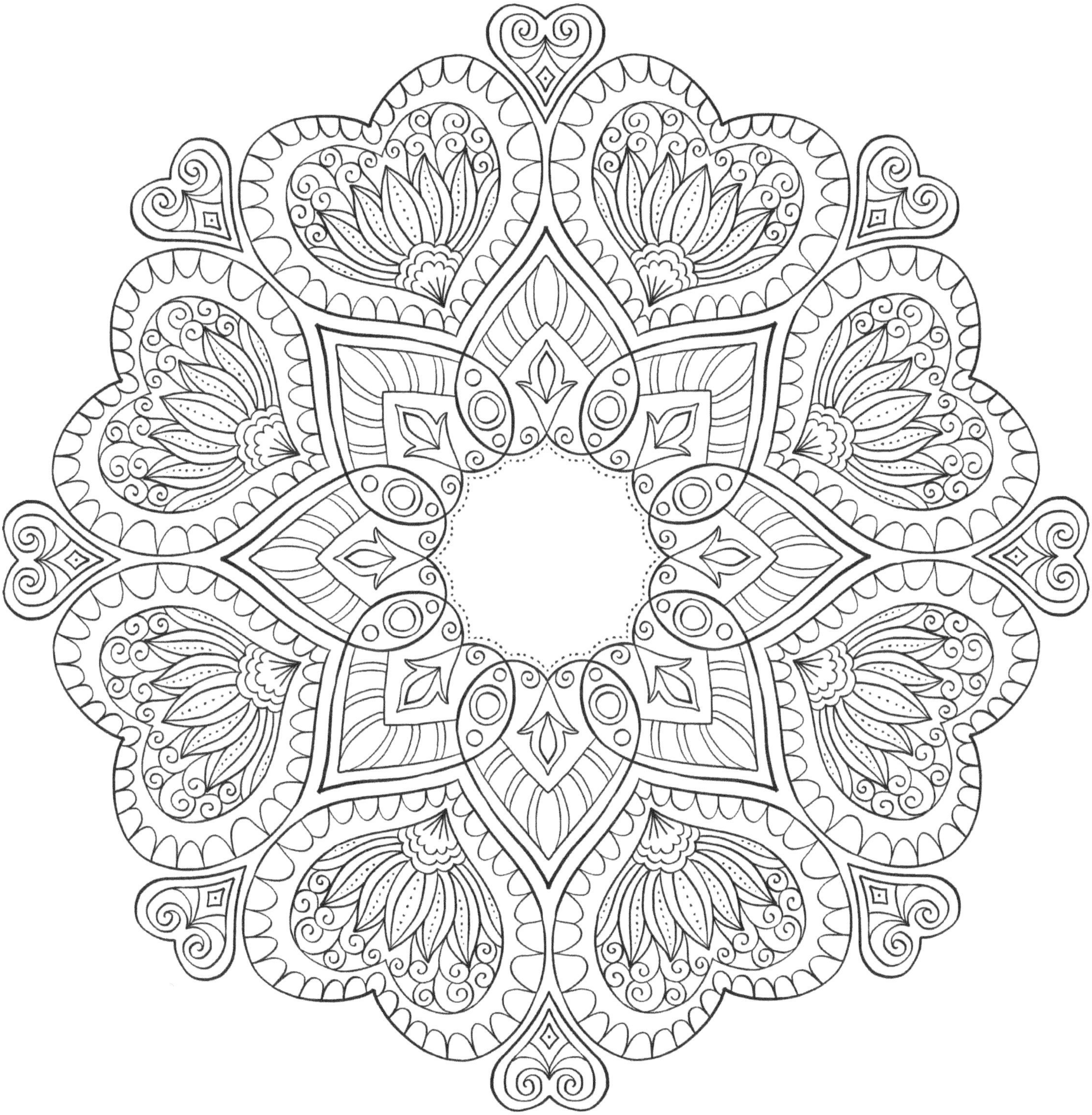

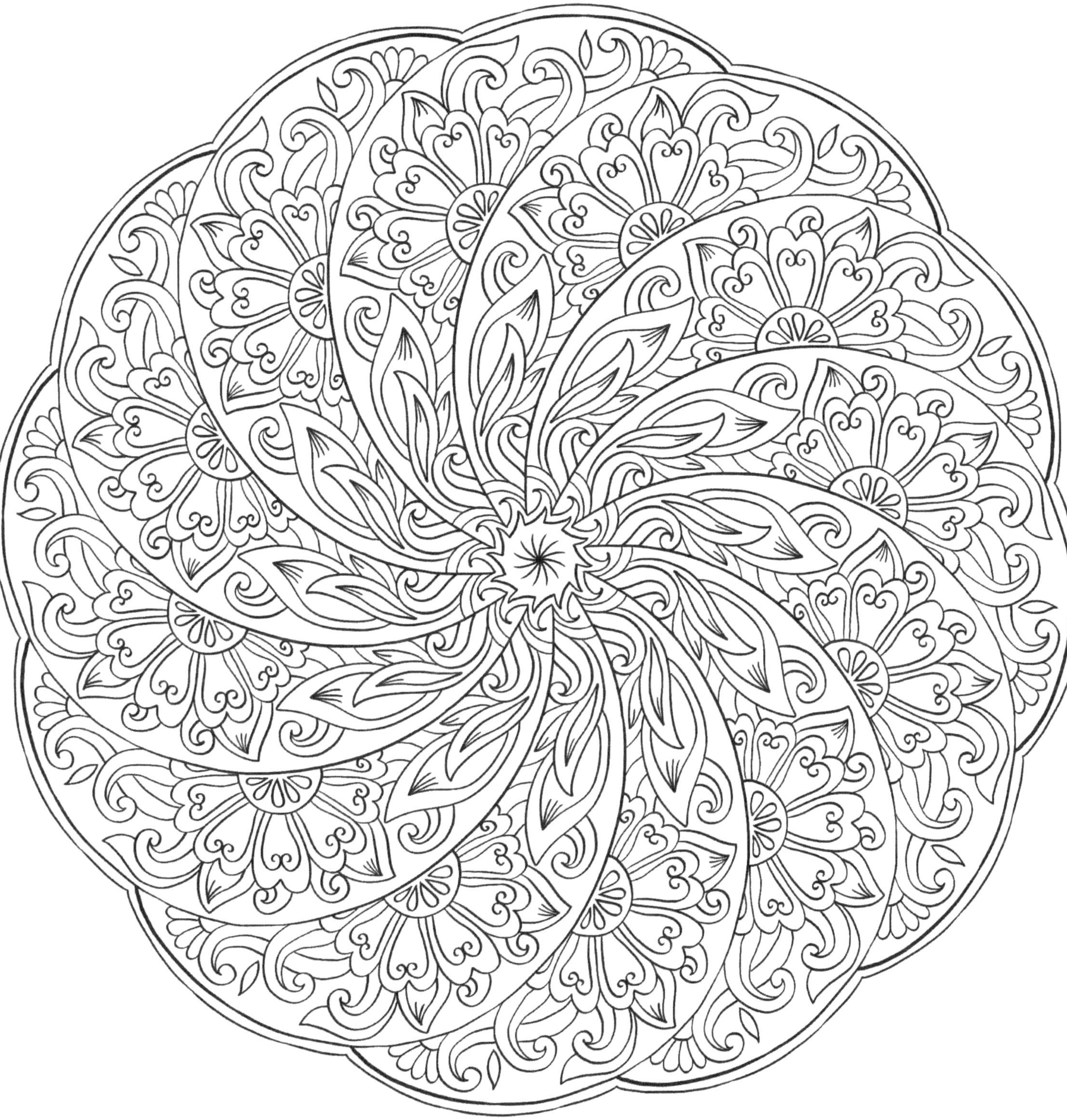

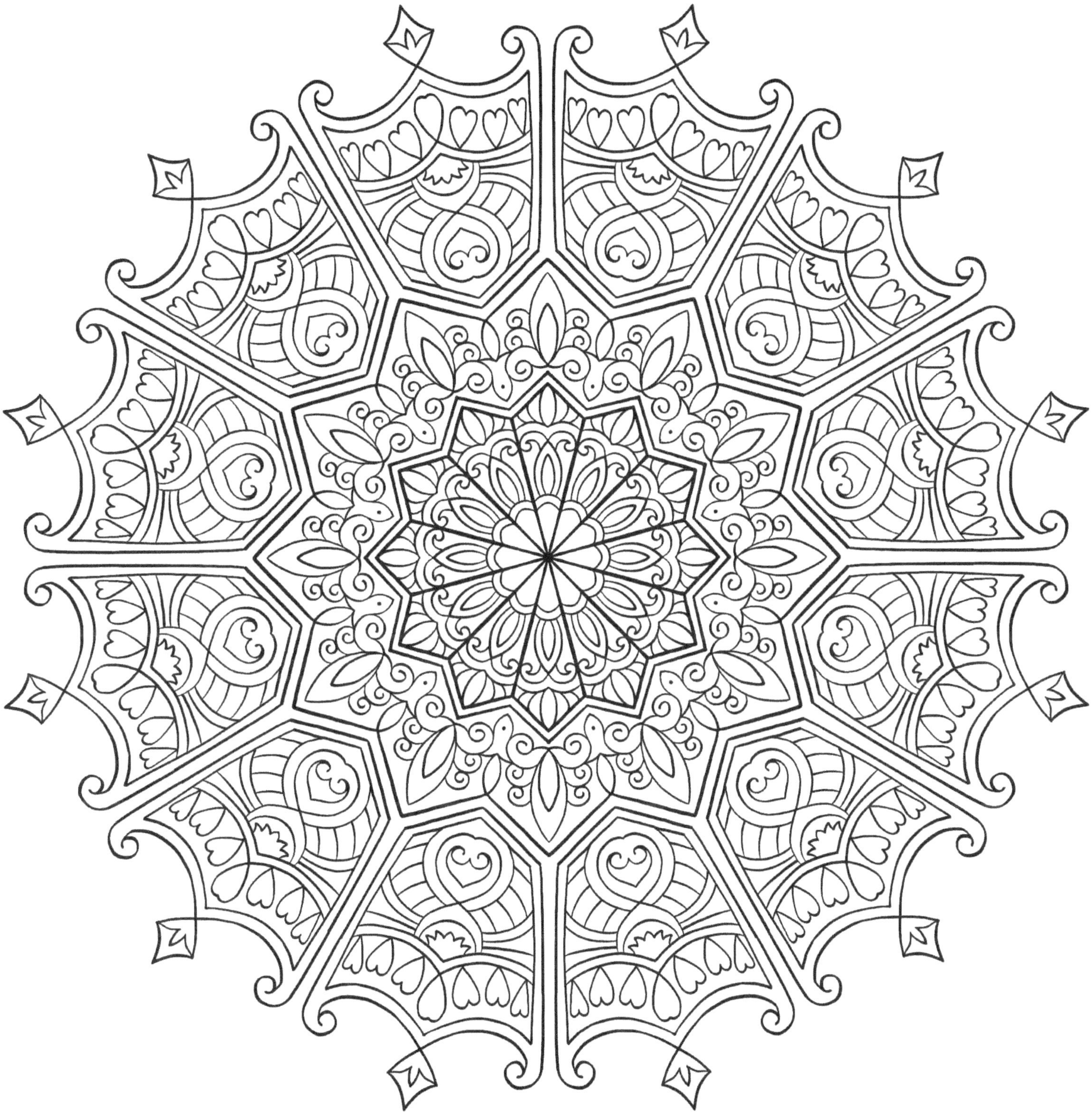

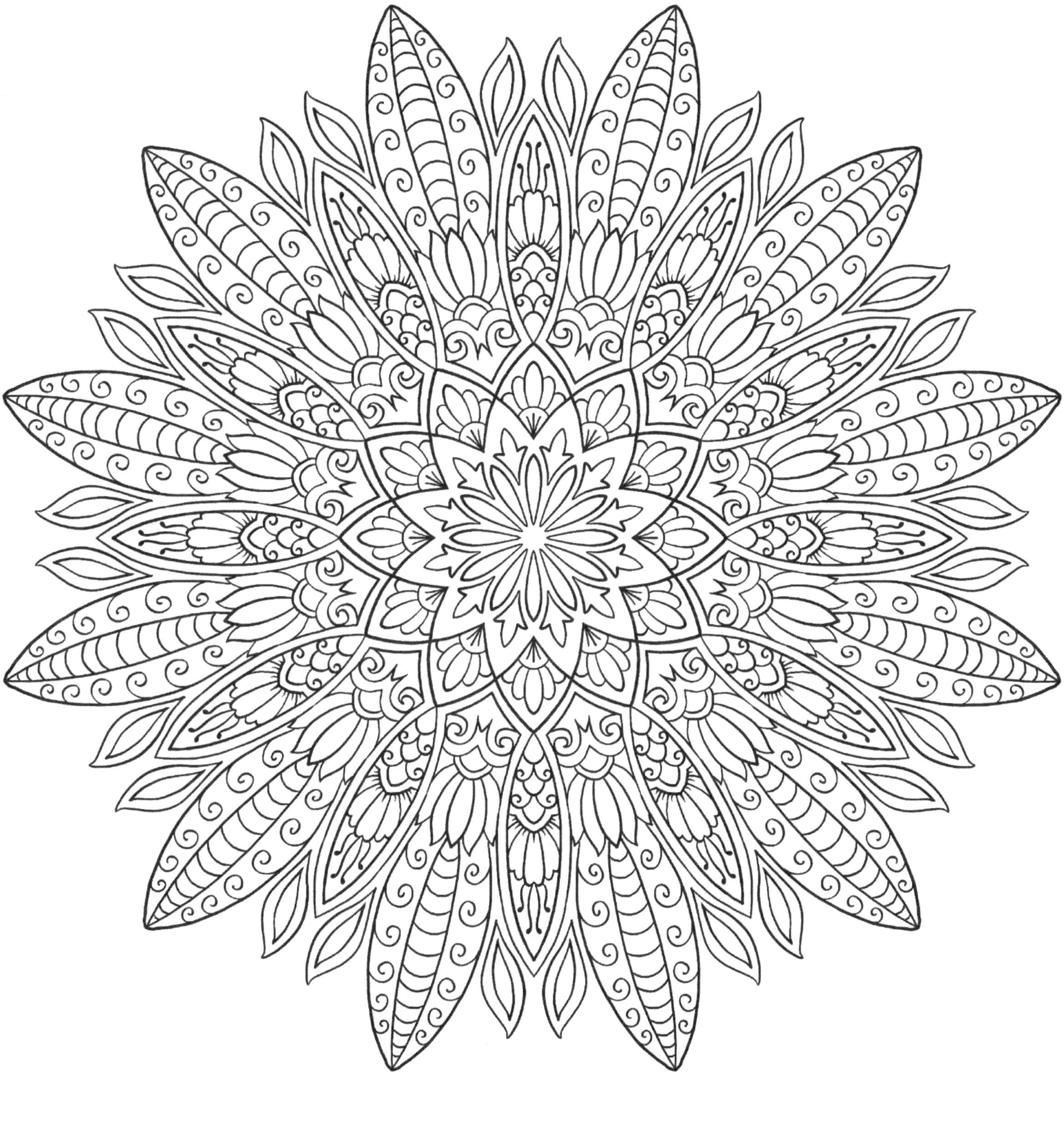

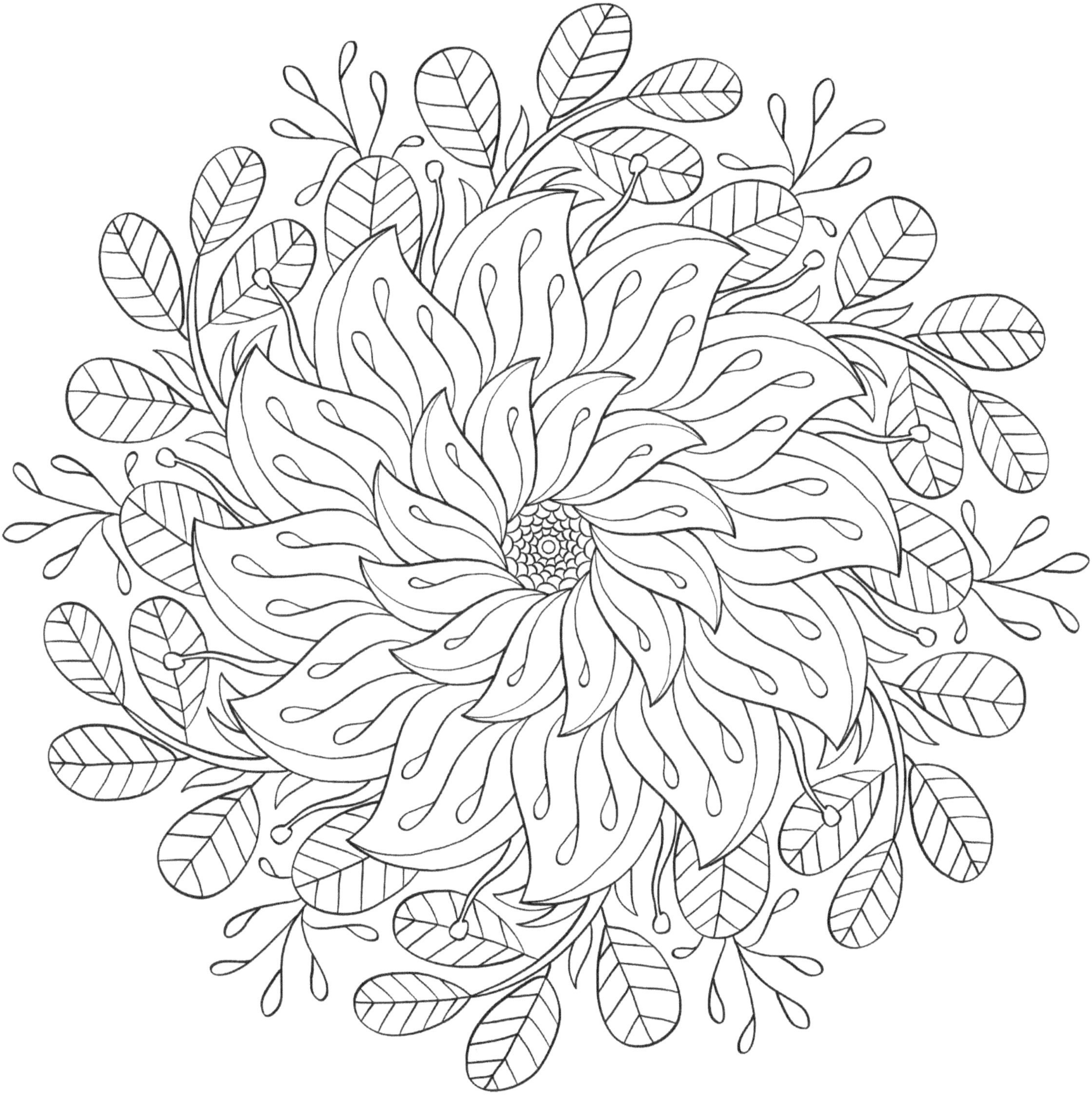

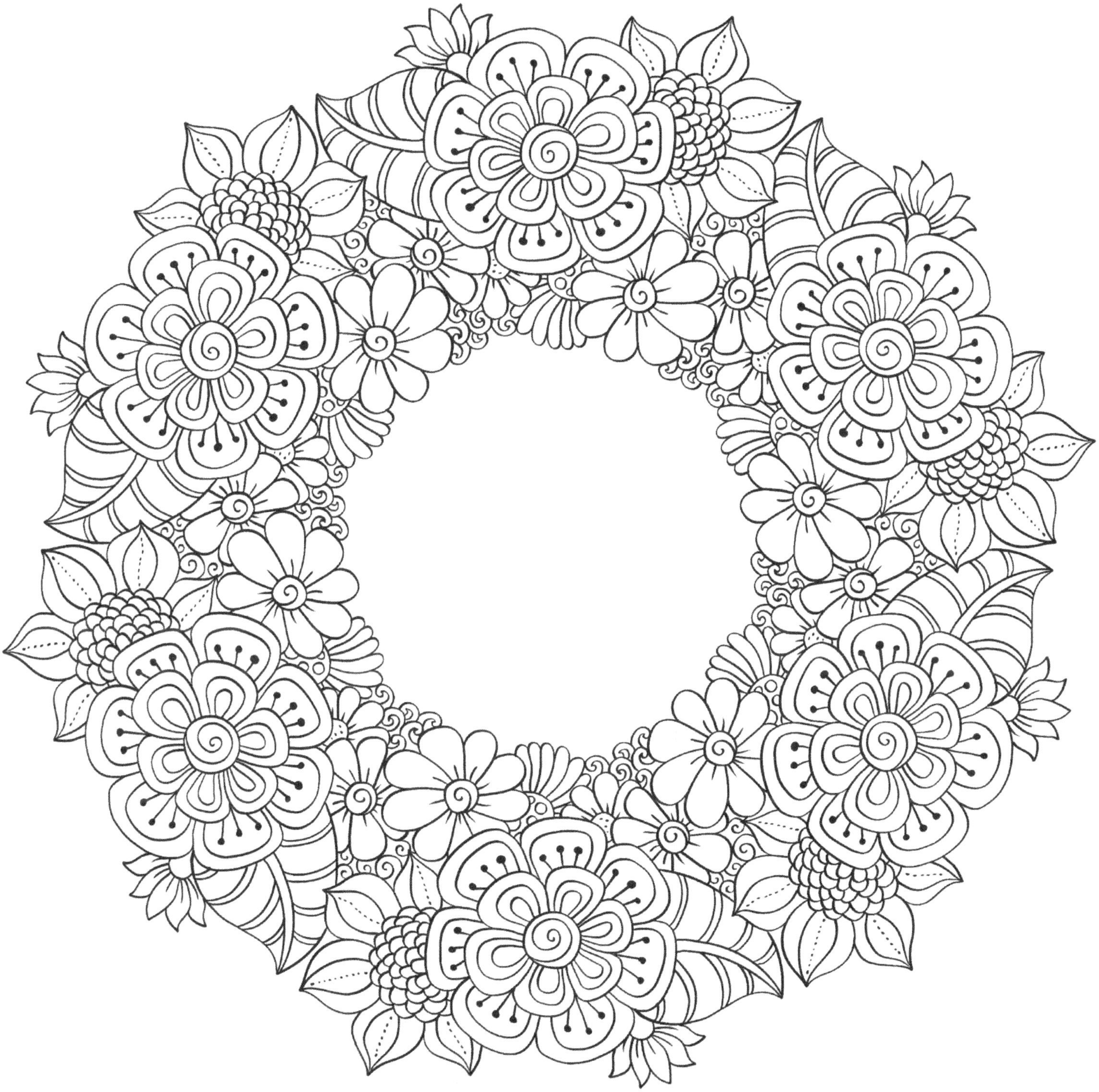

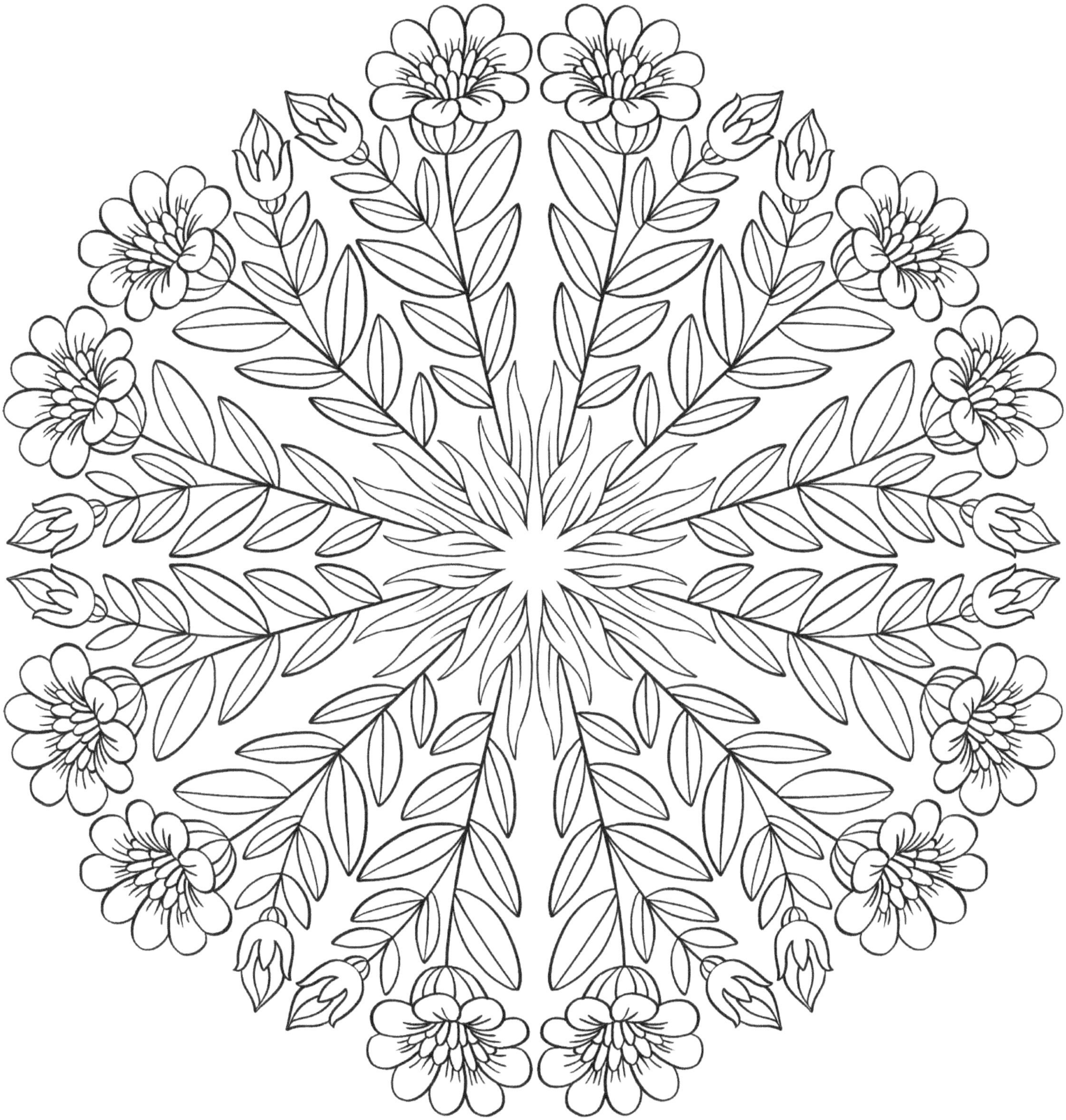

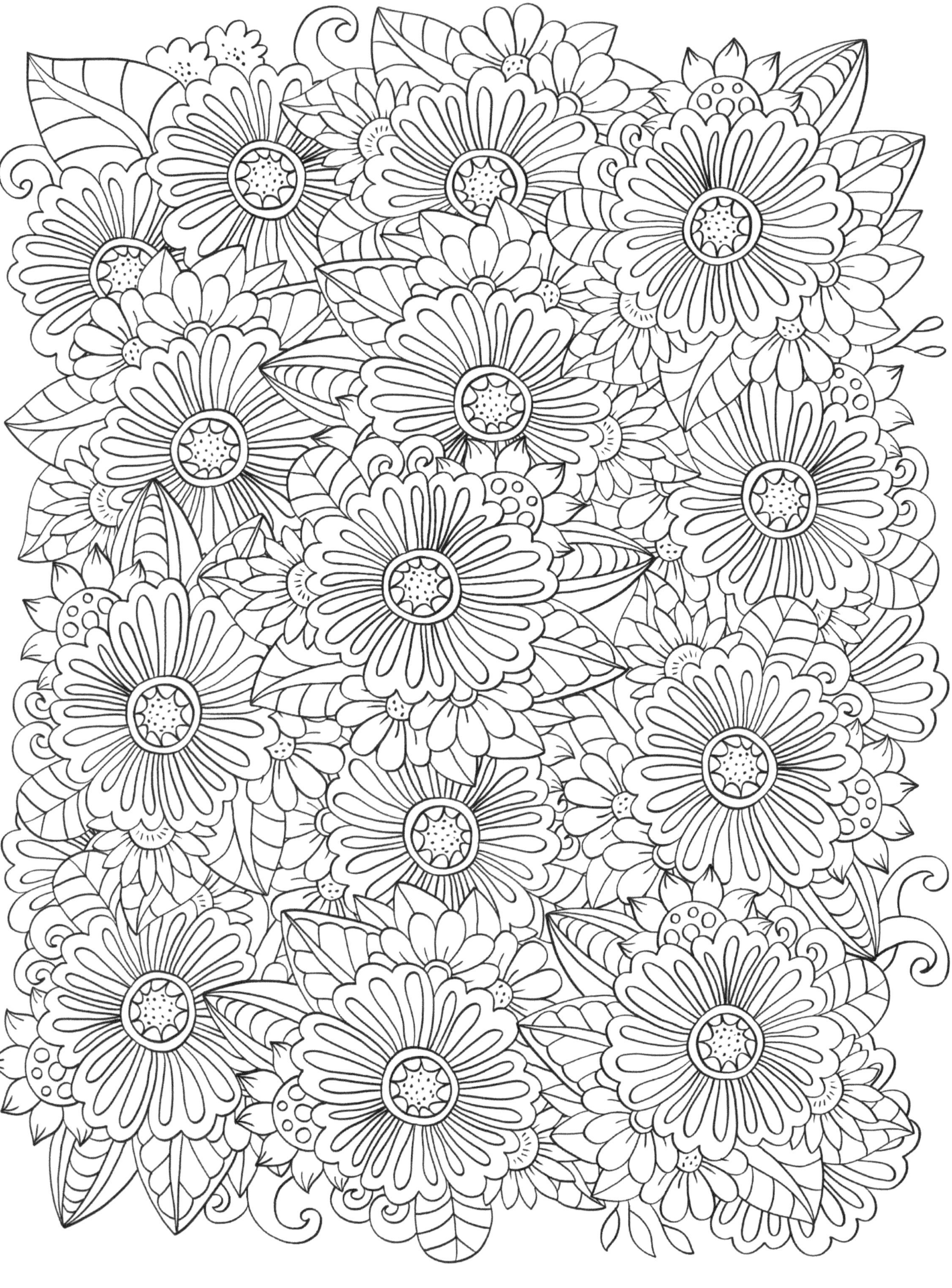

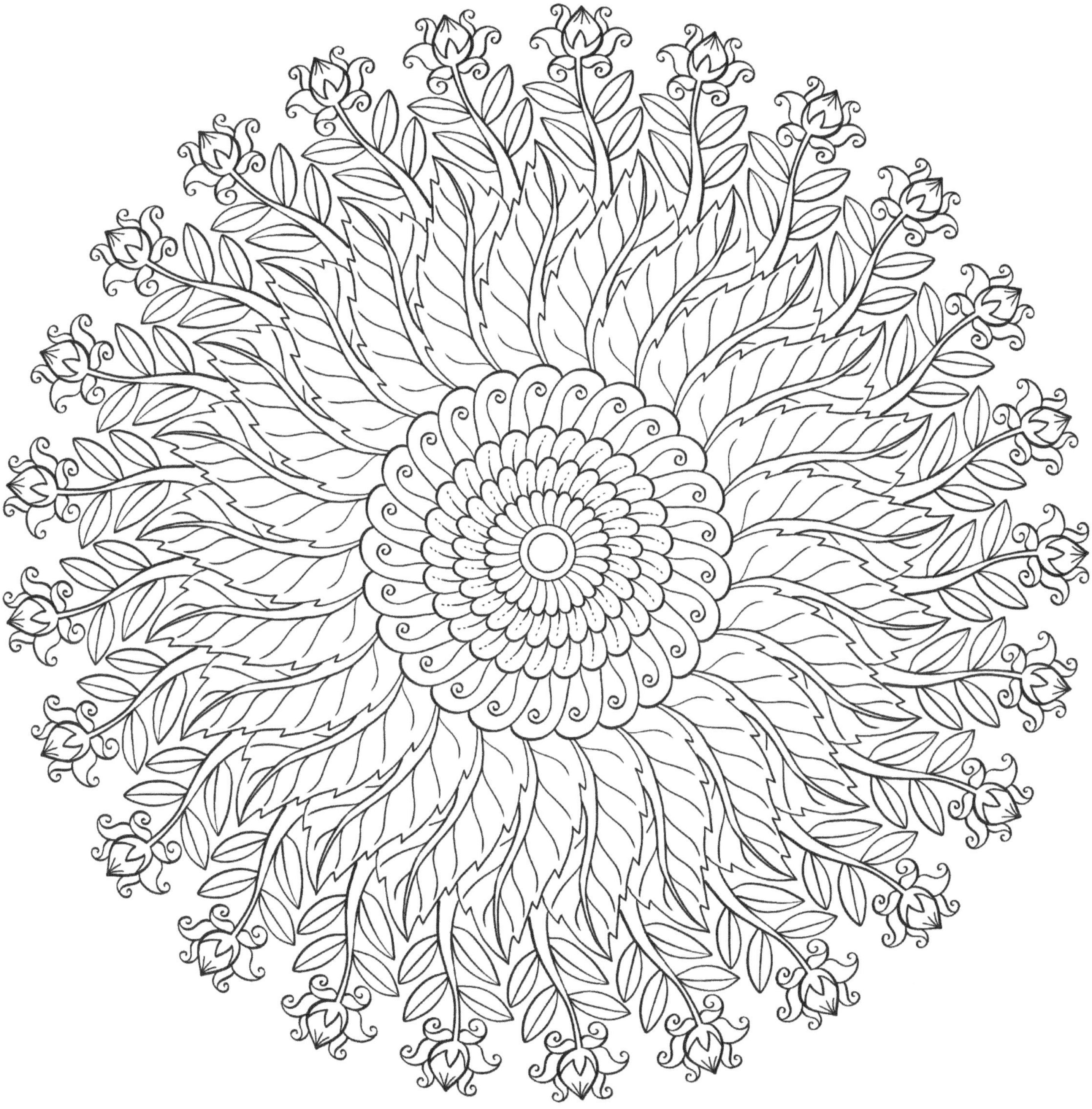

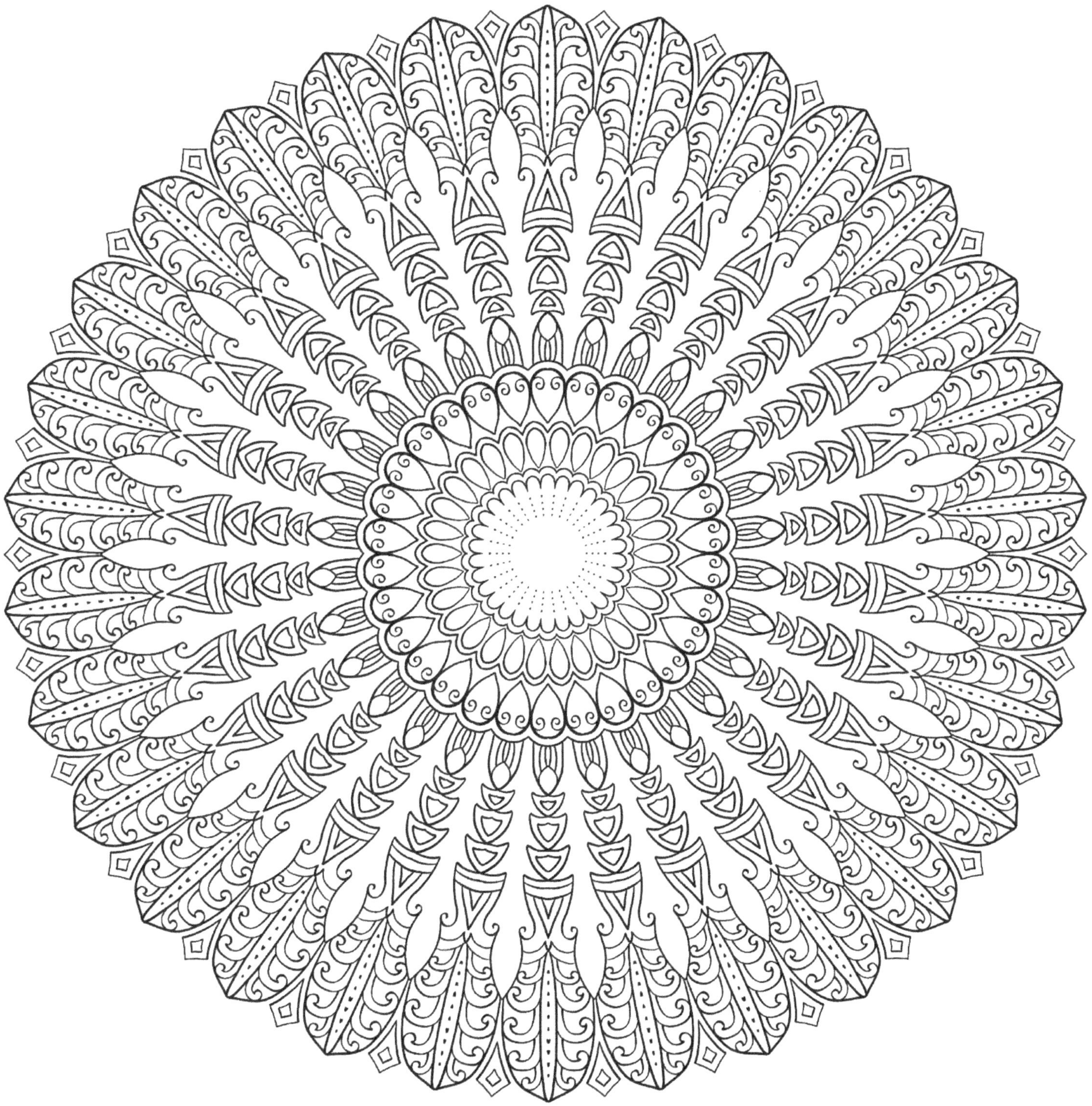

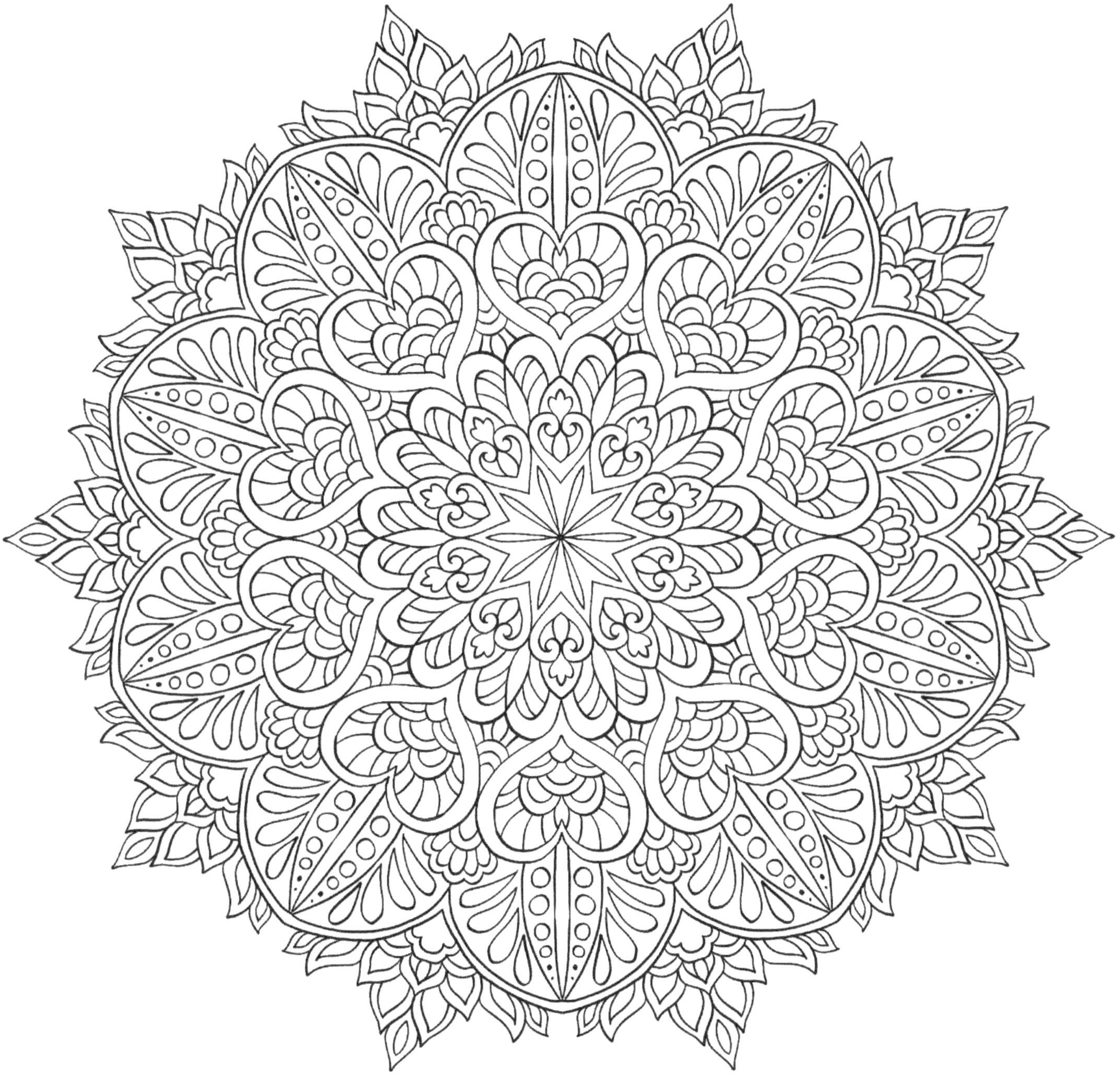

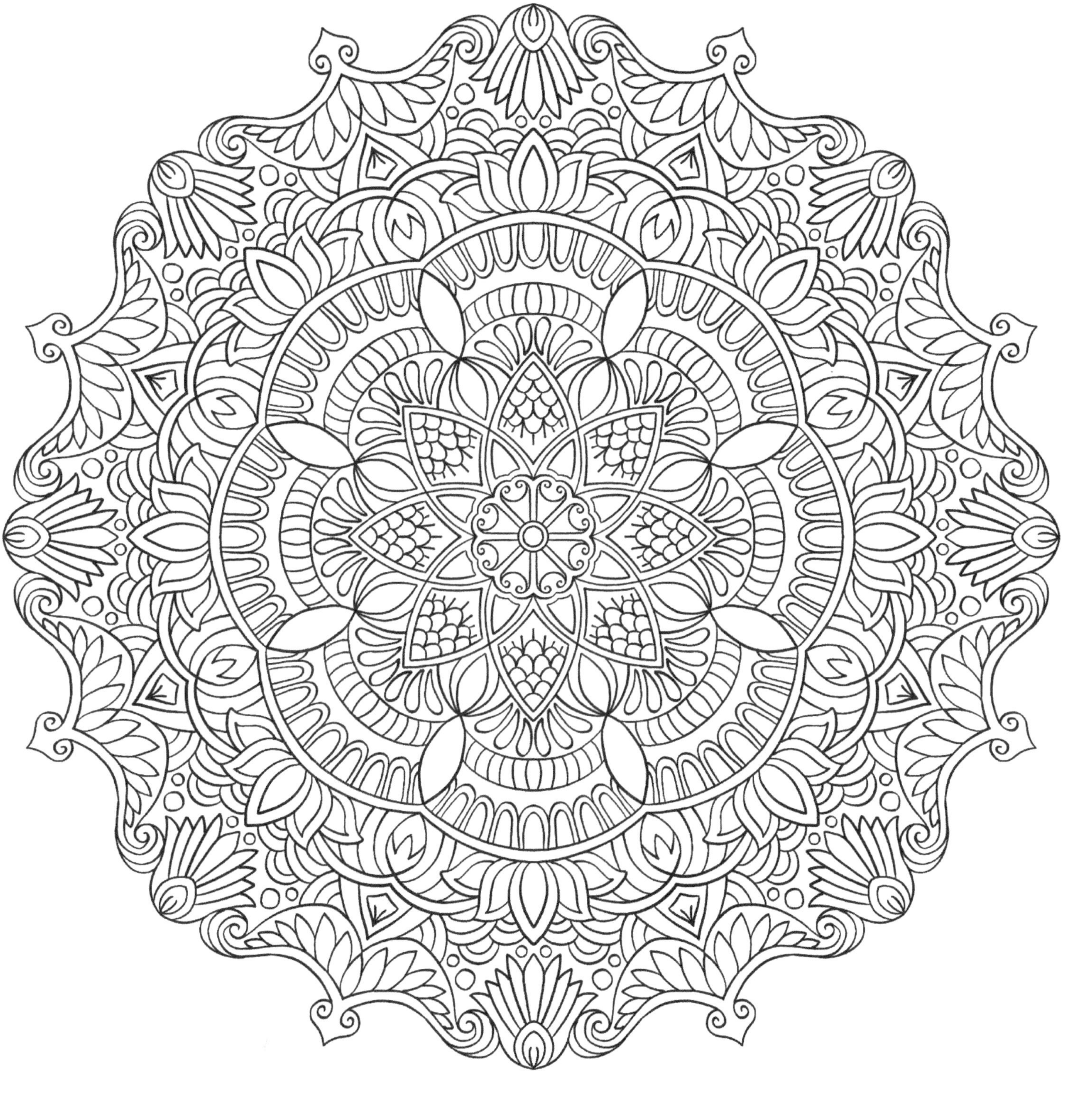

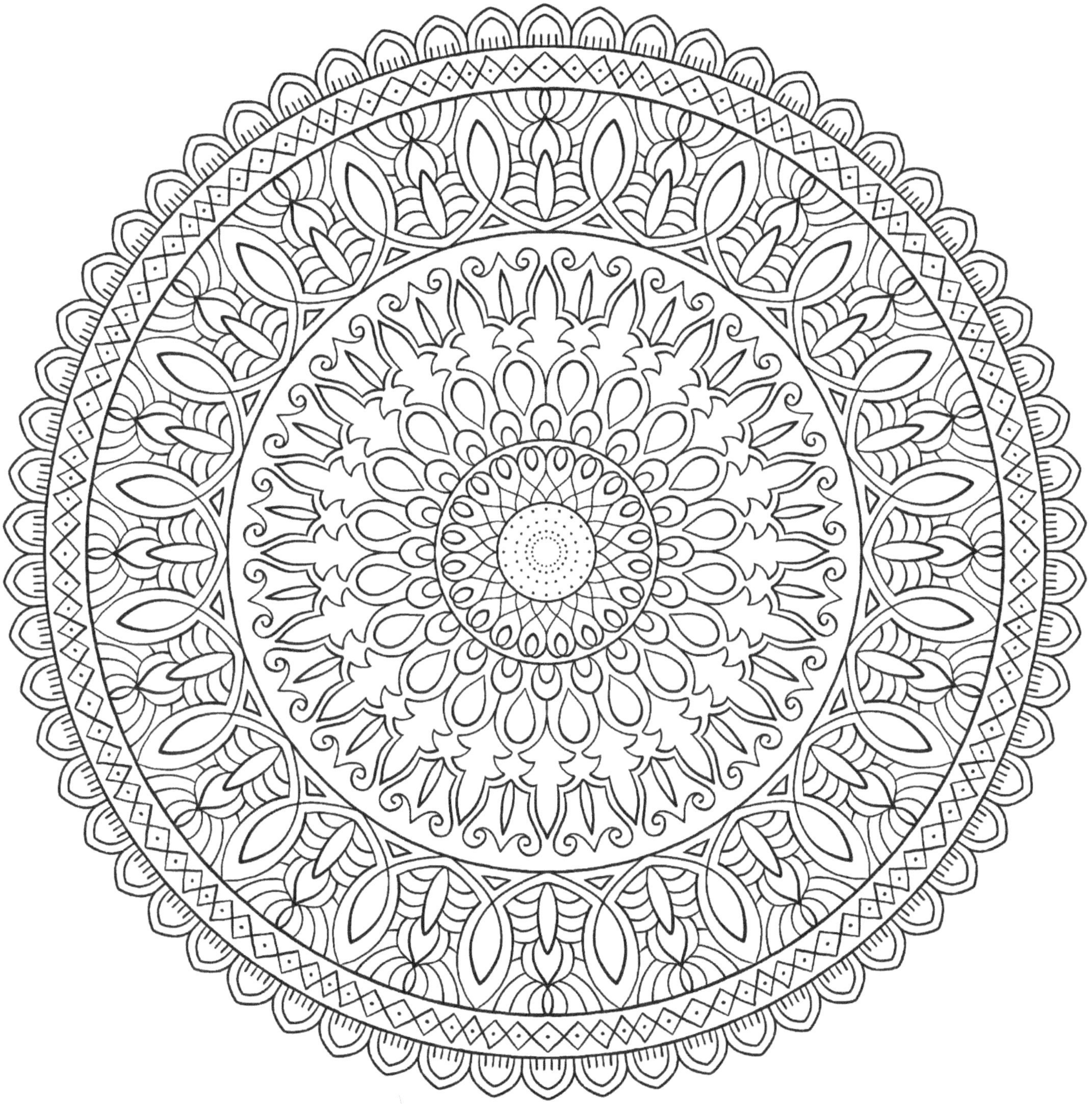

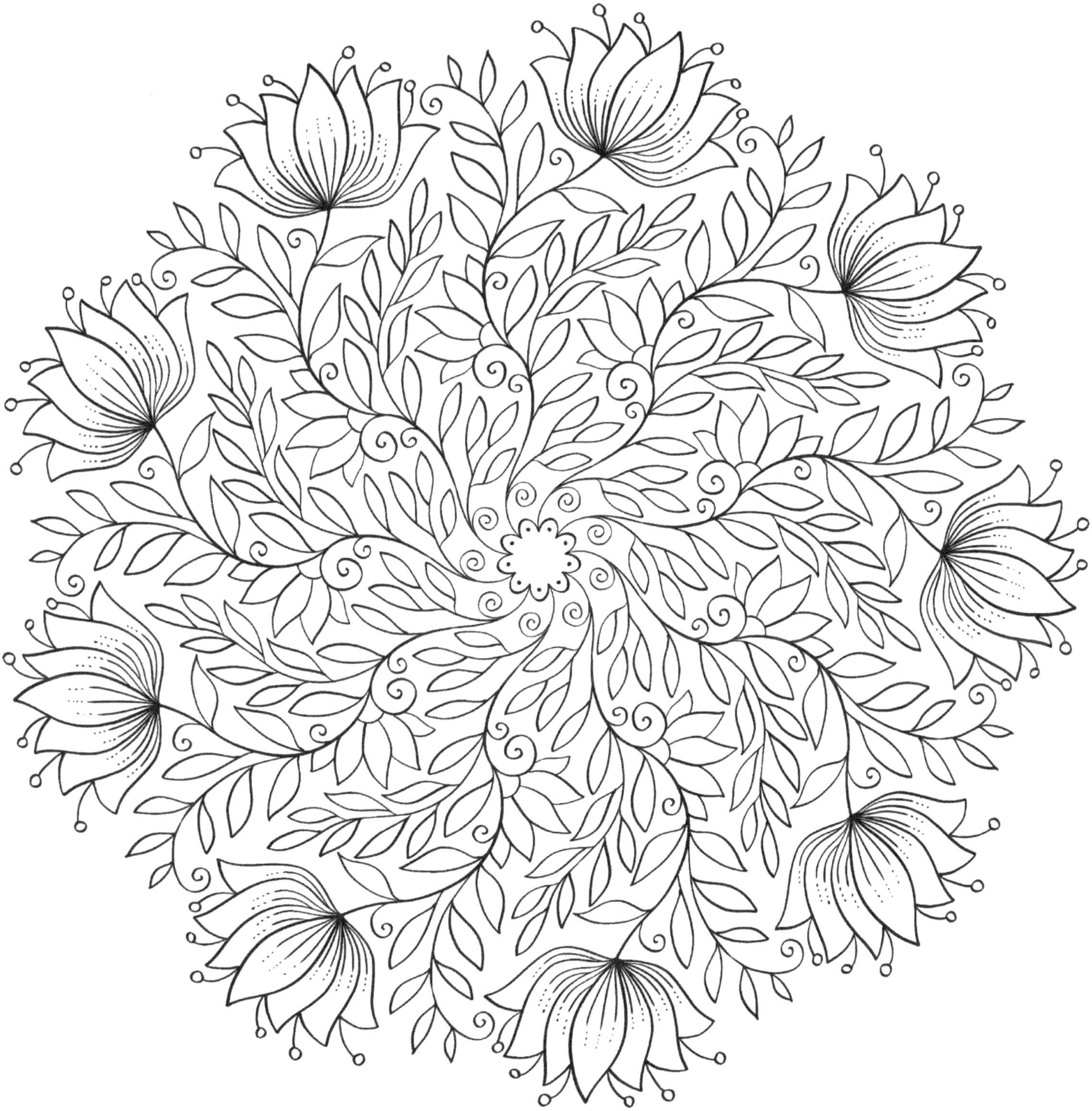

Thank you for purchasing this book.

If you would like to know more about
Aryla Publishing Books please visit:-

www.ArylaPublishing.com

Or follow us on
Facebook
Twitter
Instagram
for *free promotions*

@arylapublishing

We would love to know what you think of
this book so please leave us a review.

Have a wonderful day ☺

Other Coloring Books from Aryla Publishing

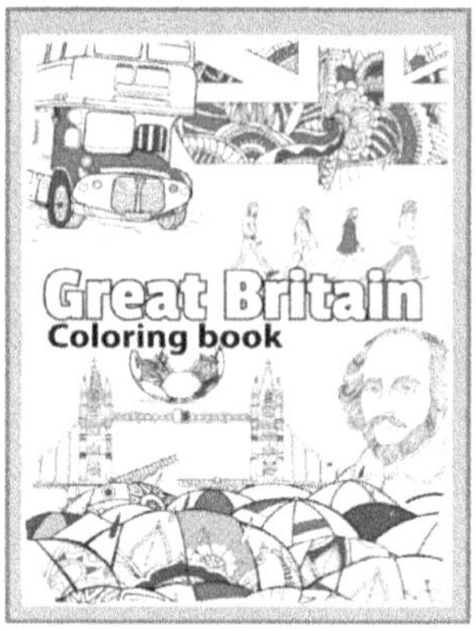

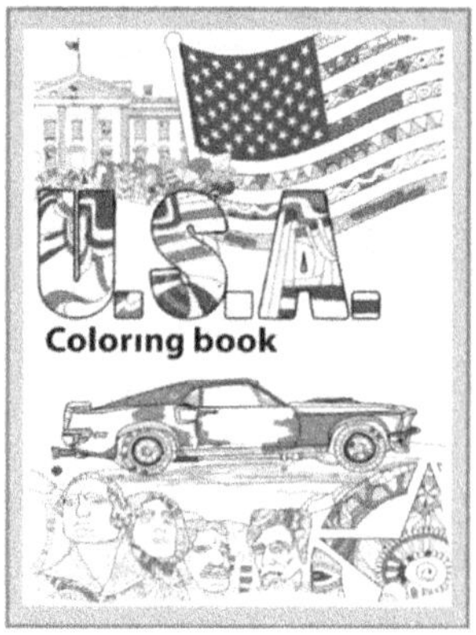

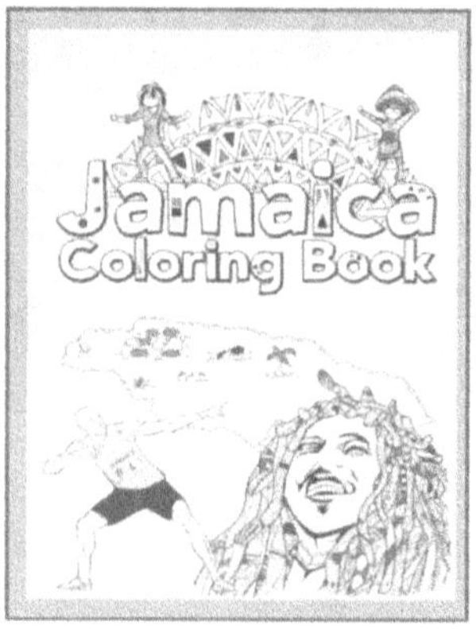

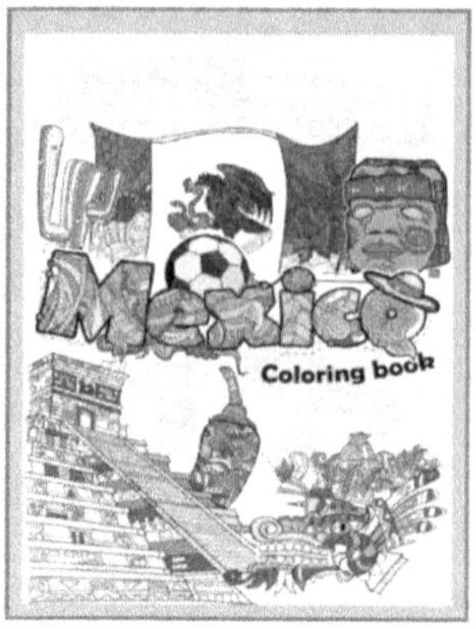

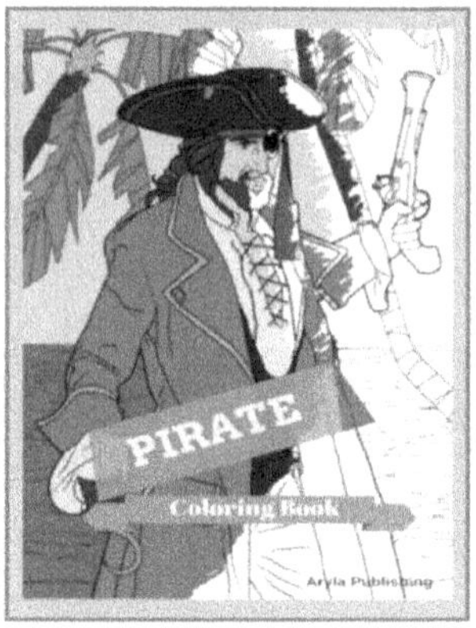

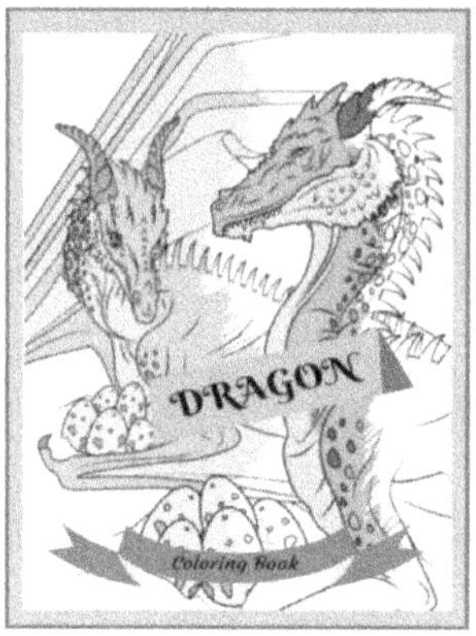

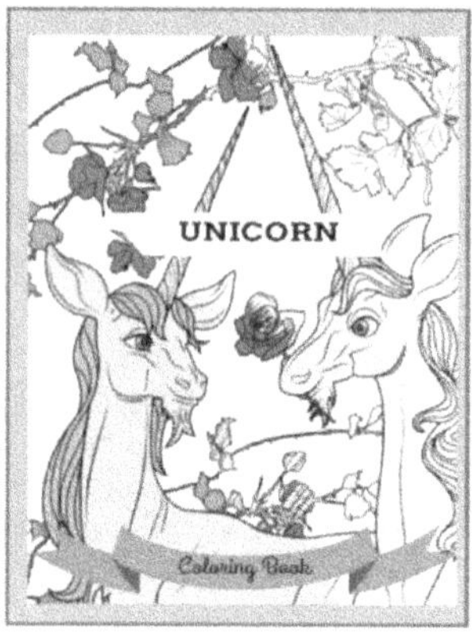

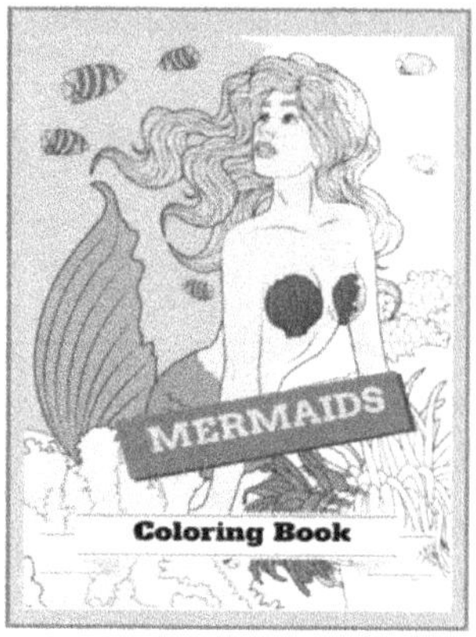

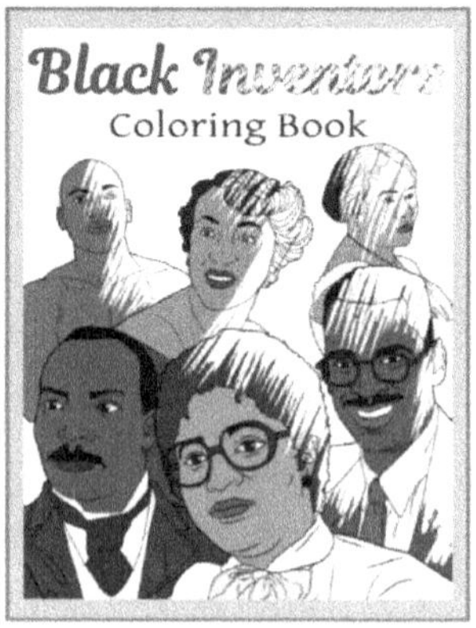

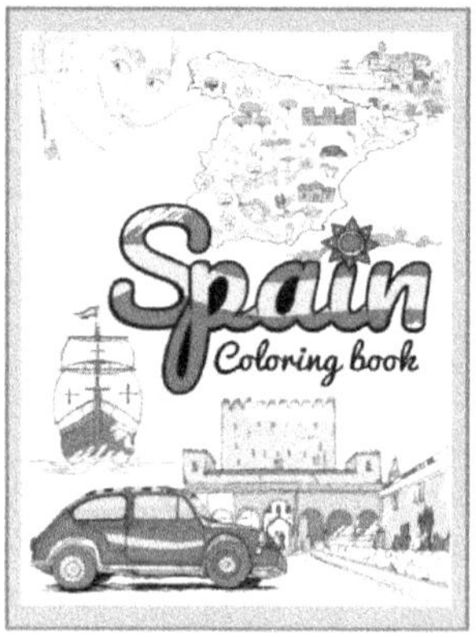

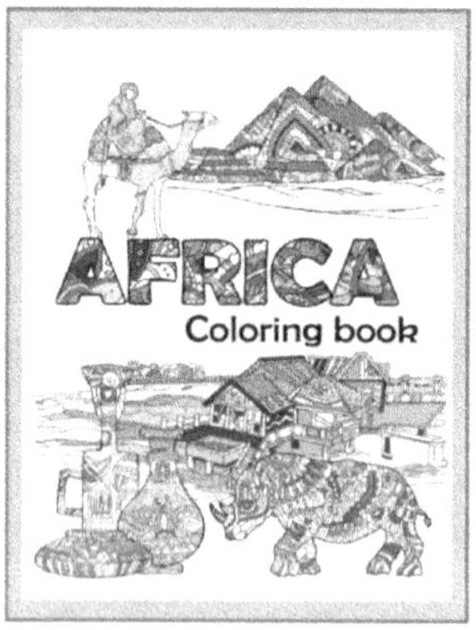

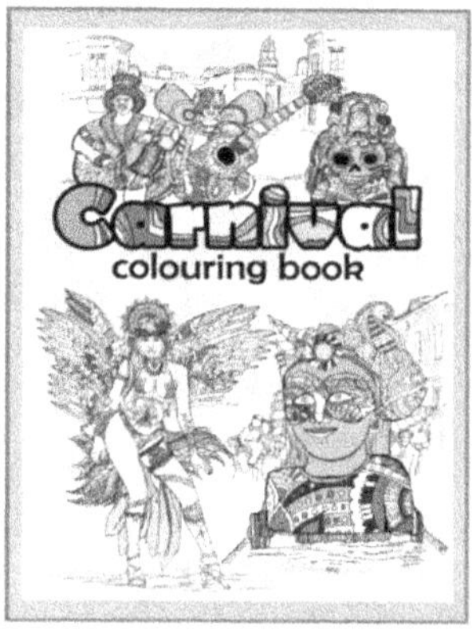

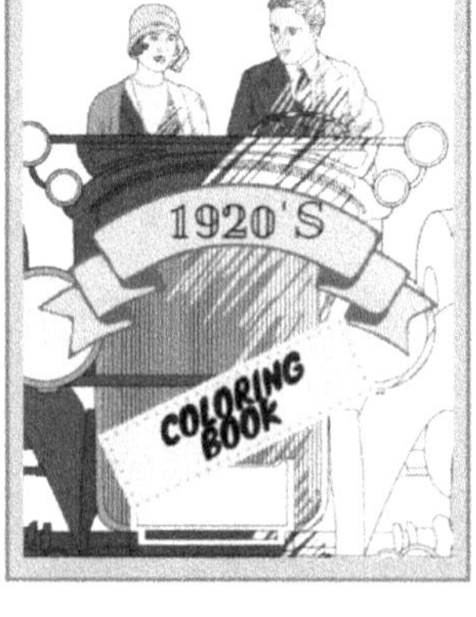

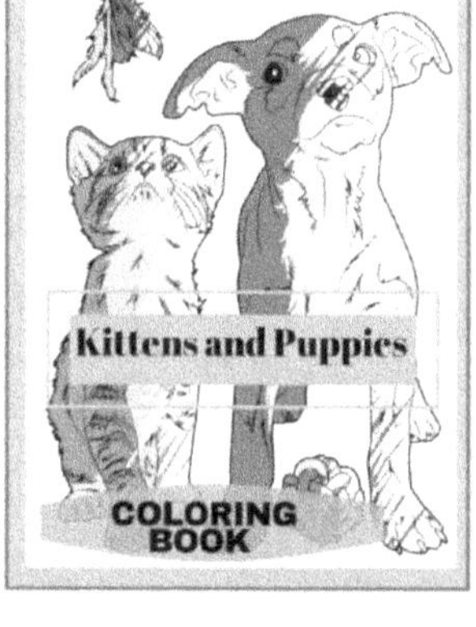

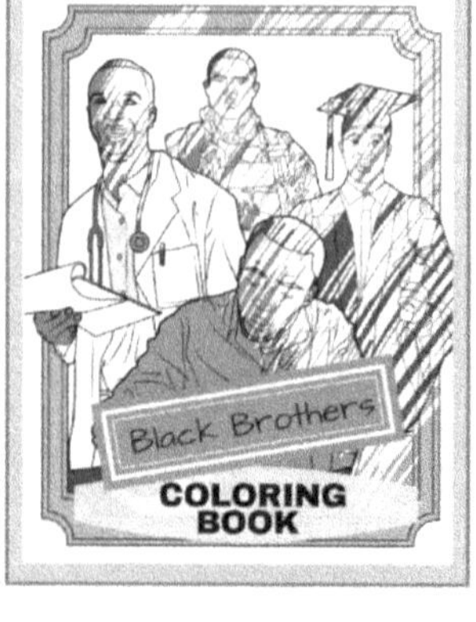

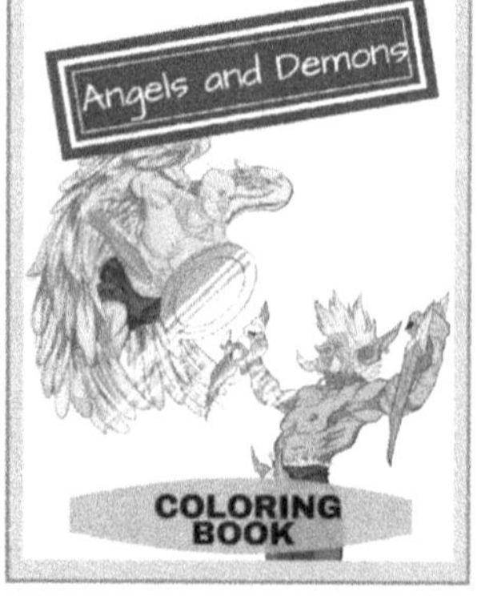

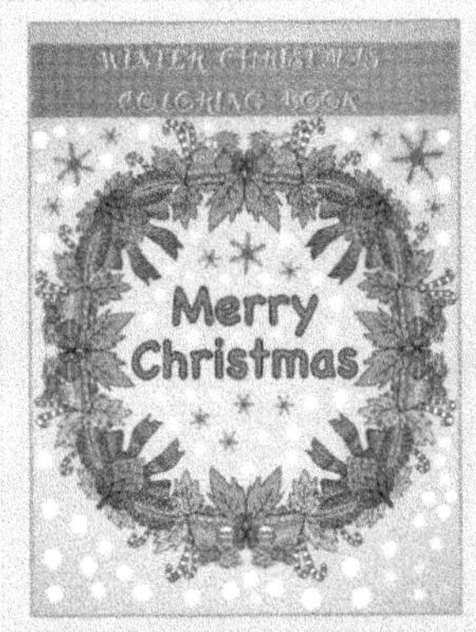
Merry Christmas

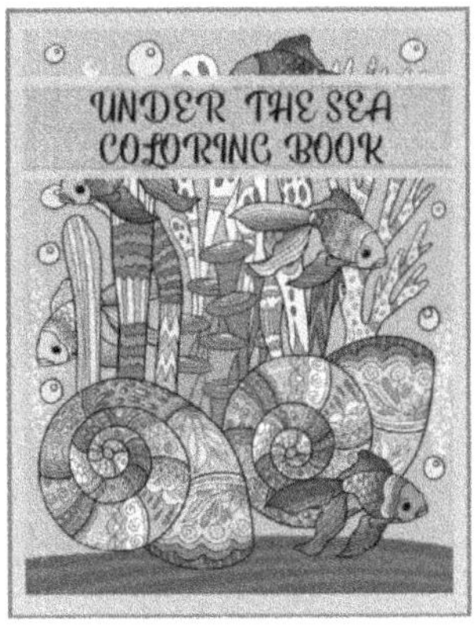
UNDER THE SEA
COLORING BOOK

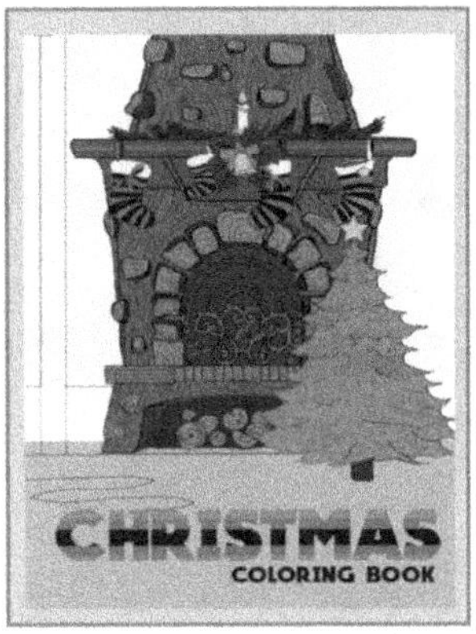
CHRISTMAS
COLORING BOOK

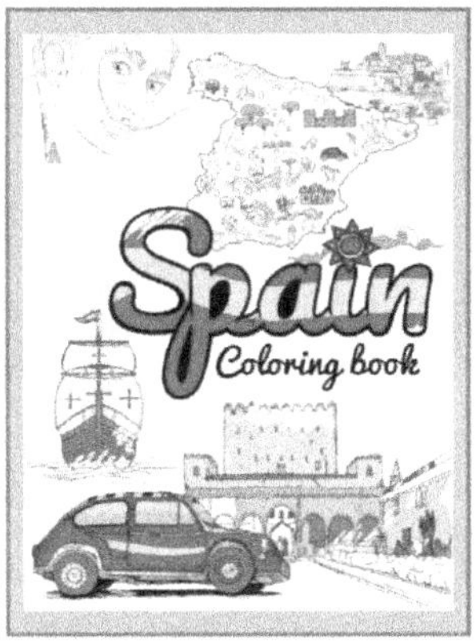
Spain
Coloring book

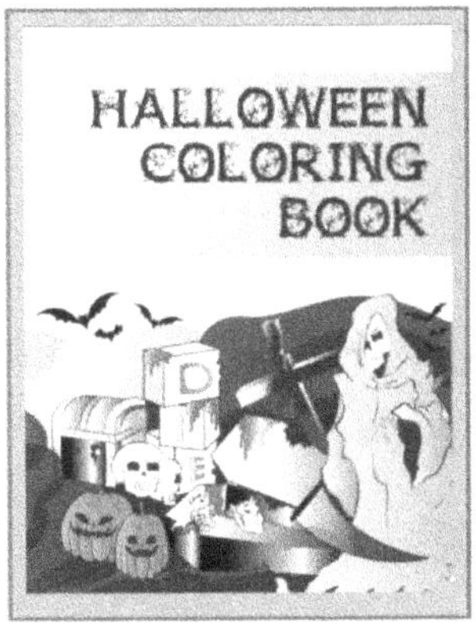
HALLOWEEN
COLORING
BOOK

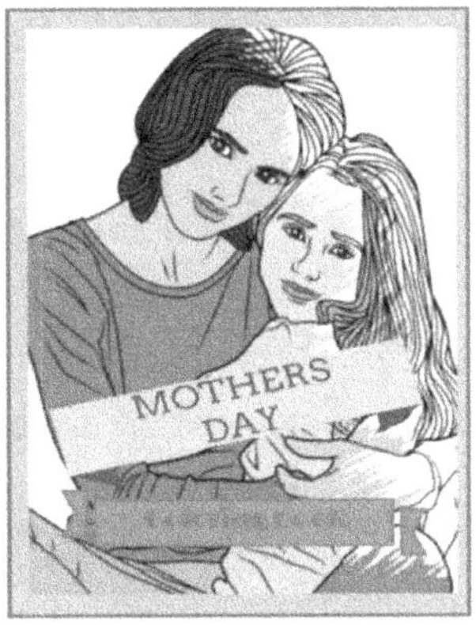
MOTHERS
DAY

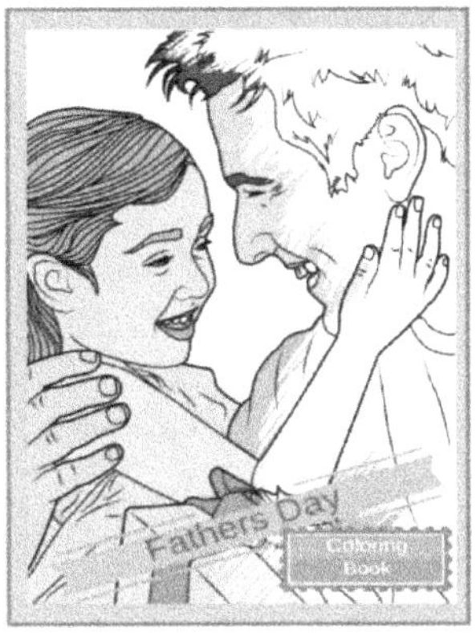
Fathers Day
Coloring
Book

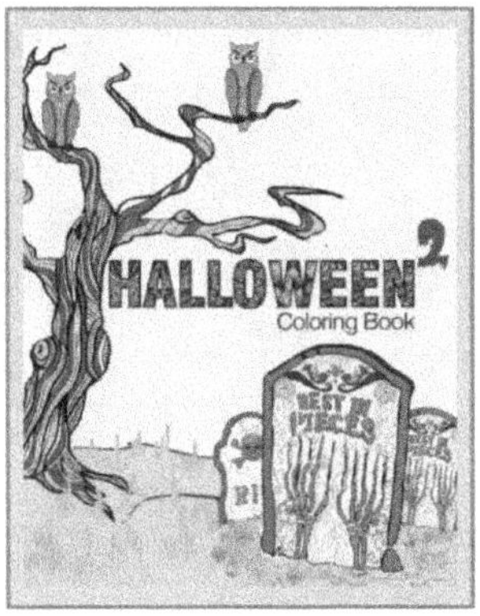
HALLOWEEN
Coloring Book

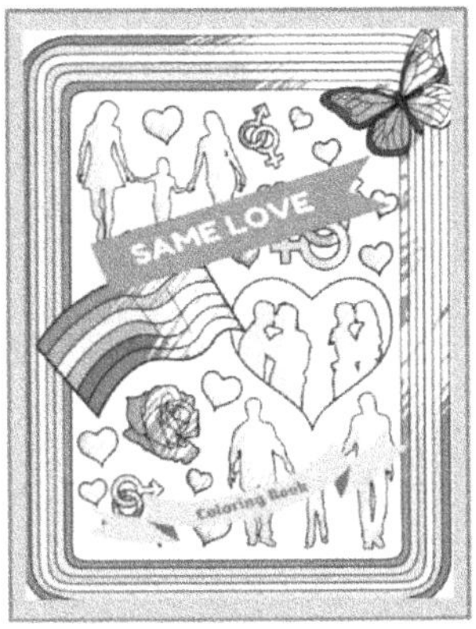
SAME LOVE
Coloring Book

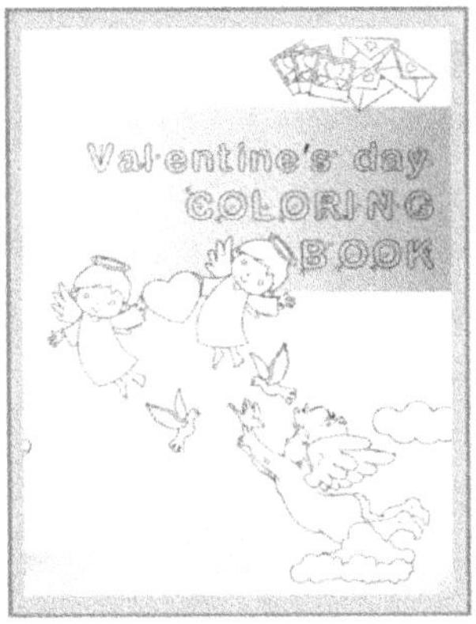
Valentine's day
COLORING
BOOK

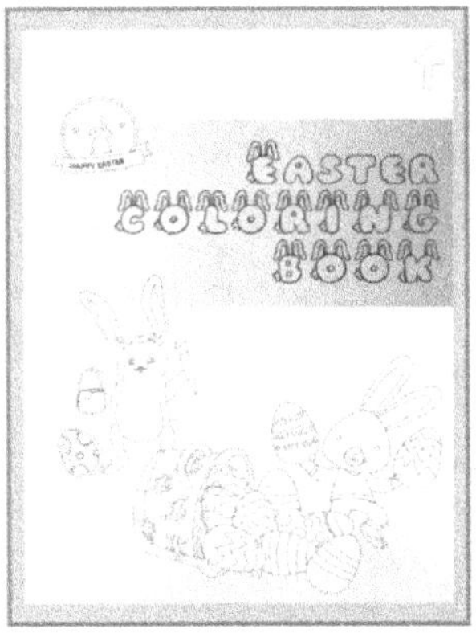
EASTER
COLORING
BOOK

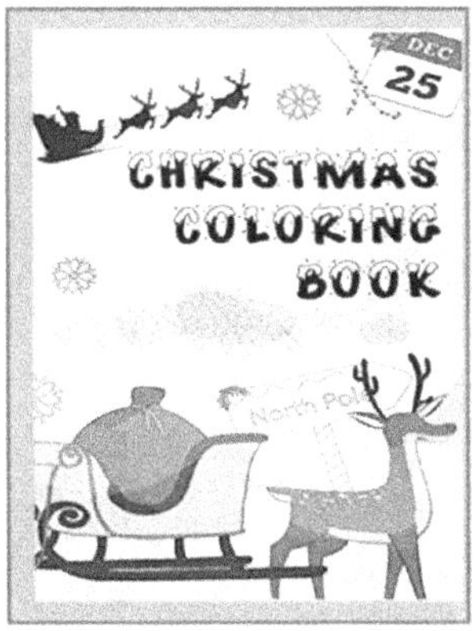
DEC
25
CHRISTMAS
COLORING
BOOK

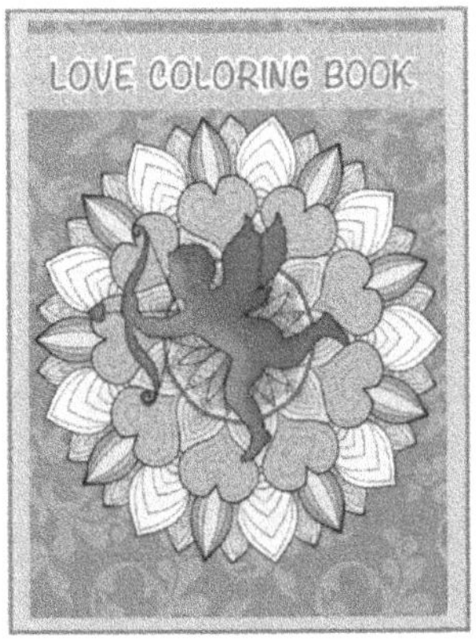
LOVE COLORING BOOK

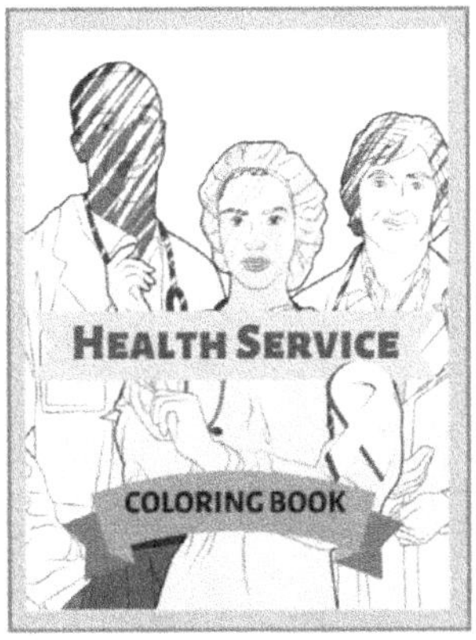
HEALTH SERVICE
COLORING BOOK

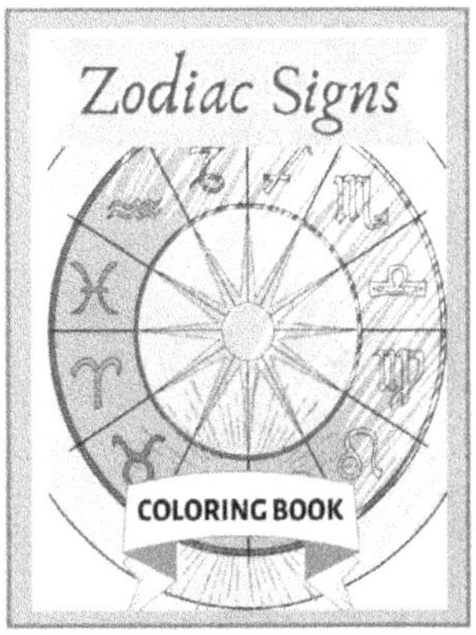
Zodiac Signs
COLORING BOOK

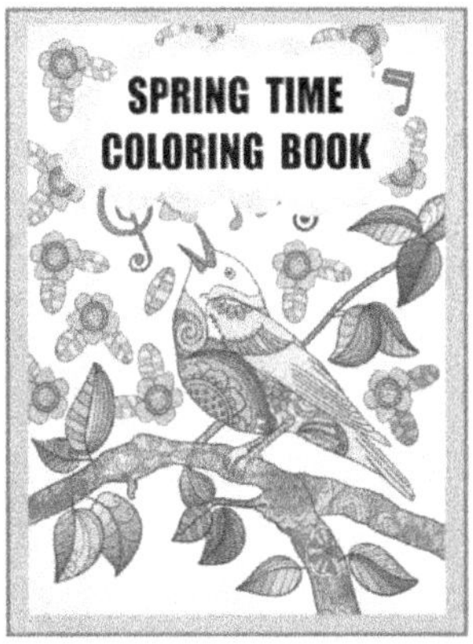
SPRING TIME
COLORING BOOK

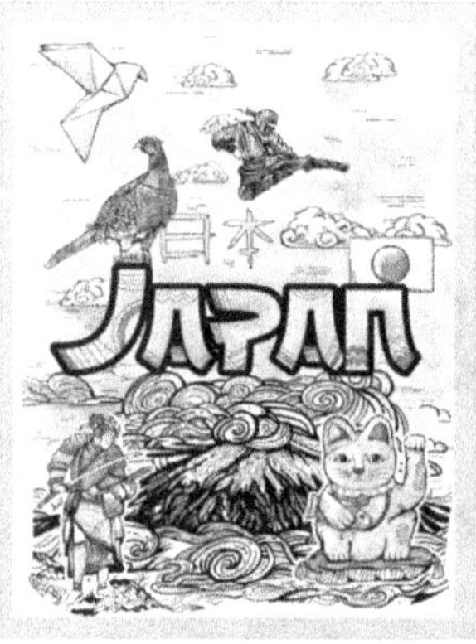
JAPAN

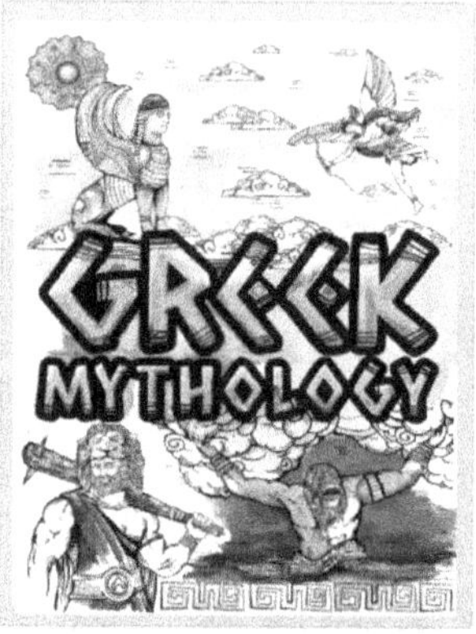
GREEK
MYTHOLOGY

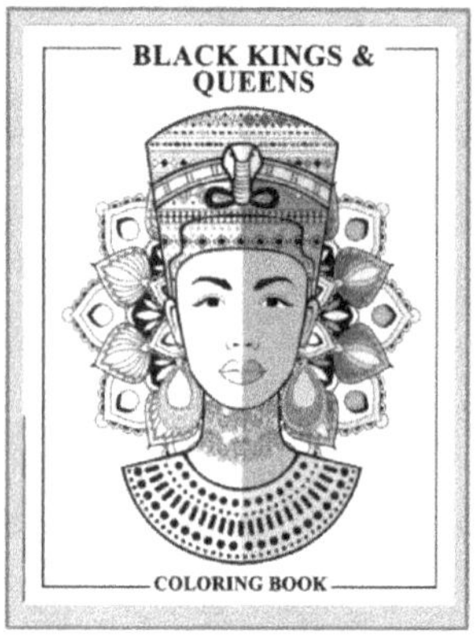
BLACK KINGS &
QUEENS
COLORING BOOK

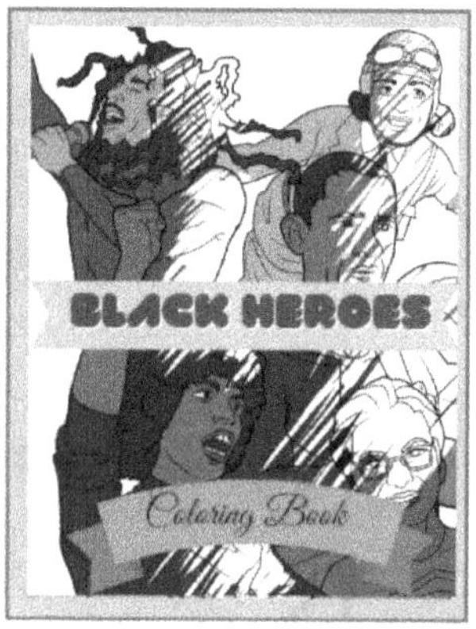
BLACK HEROES
Coloring Book

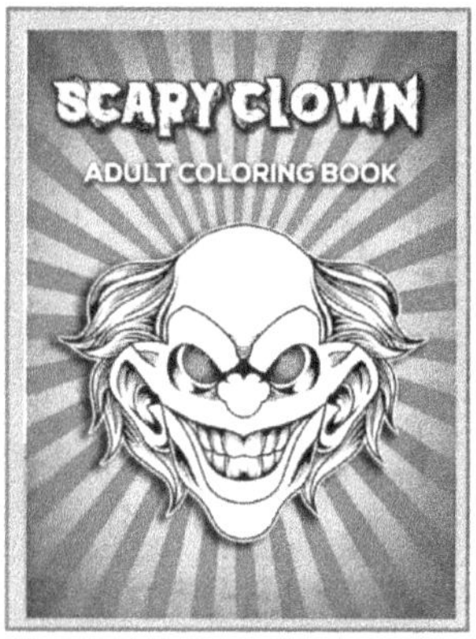
SCARY CLOWN
ADULT COLORING BOOK

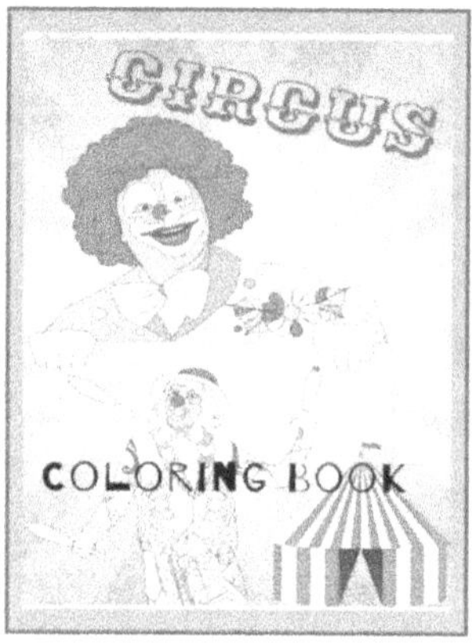
CIRCUS
COLORING BOOK

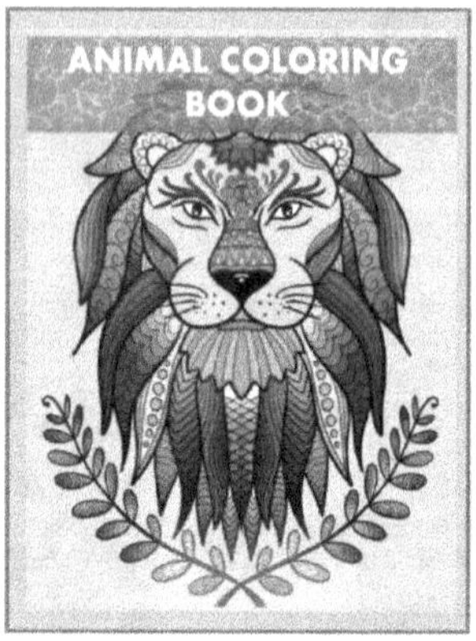
ANIMAL COLORING
BOOK

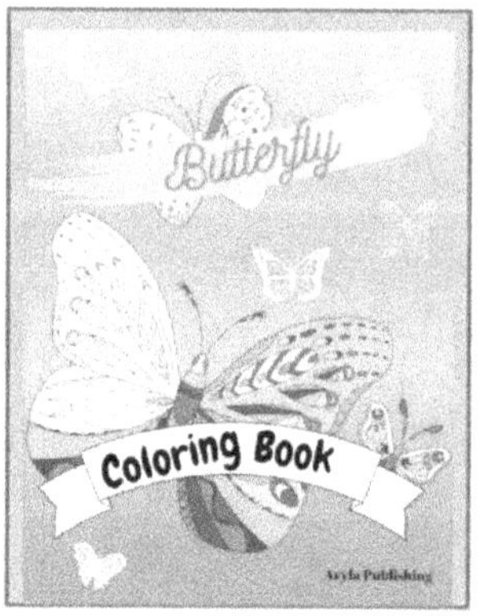
Butterfly
Coloring Book

Color In Fun
Kids Books

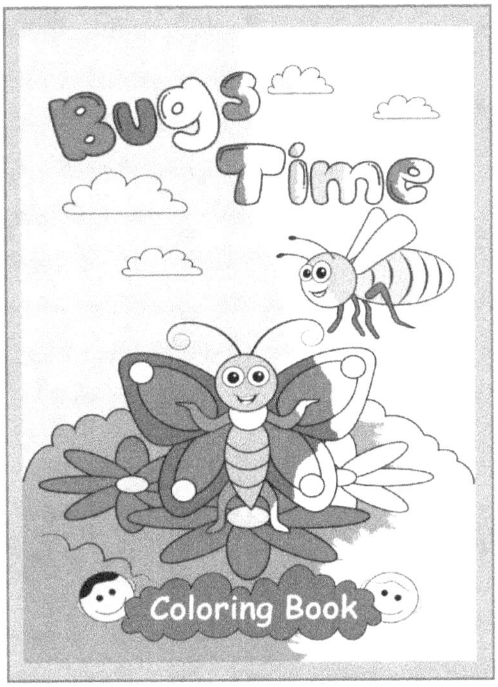

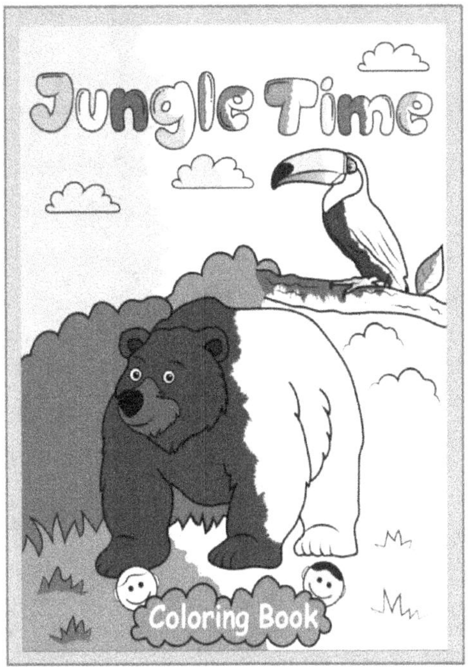

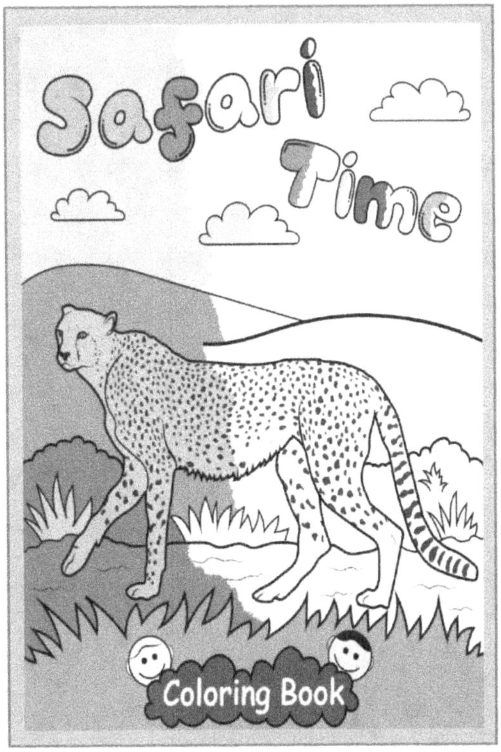

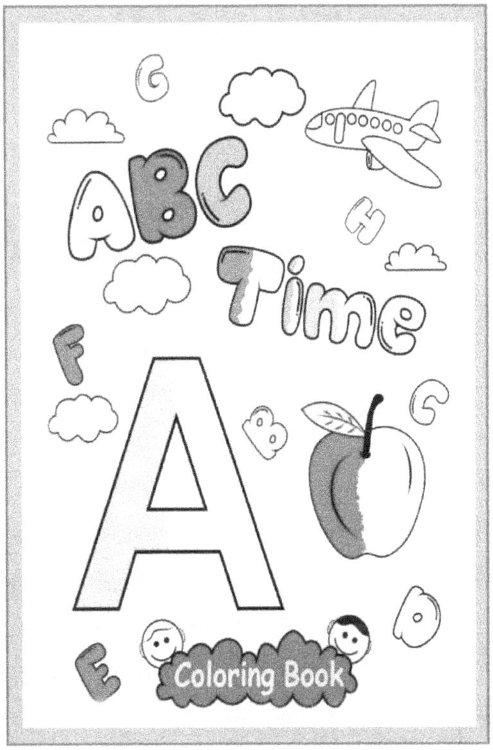

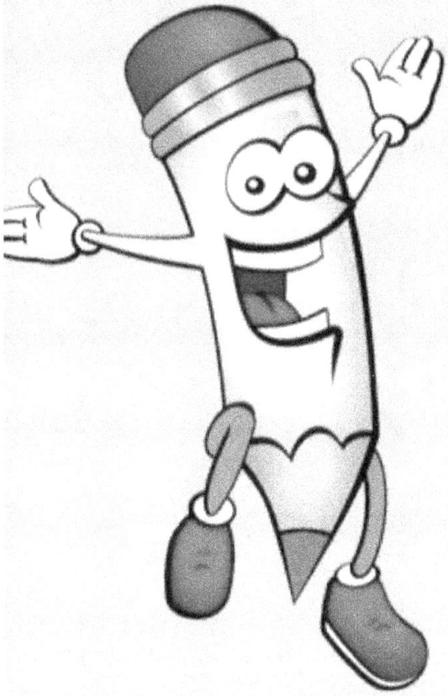

WE WOULD LOVE YOUR FEEDBACK

PLEASE LEAVE REVIEW AT:-

www.ingramcontent.com/pod-product-compliance
Lightning Source LLC
Chambersburg PA
CBHW080133240526
45468CB00009BA/2400
9781912675845